C000264736

ARISE

and

SHINE

F. Saliki

Frank Saliki

**Grosvenor House
Publishing Limited**

All rights reserved
Copyright © Frank Saliki, 2017

The right of Frank Saliki to be identified as the author of this
work has been asserted in accordance with Section 78
of the Copyright, Designs and Patents Act 1988

The book cover picture is copyright to Frank Saliki

This book is published by
Grosvenor House Publishing Ltd
Link House
140 The Broadway, Tolworth, Surrey, KT6 7HT.
www.grosvenorhousepublishing.co.uk

This book is sold subject to the conditions that it shall not, by way of
trade or otherwise, be lent, resold, hired out or otherwise circulated
without the author's or publisher's prior consent in any form of binding or
cover other than that in which it is published and
without a similar condition including this condition being imposed
on the subsequent purchaser.

A CIP record for this book
is available from the British Library

ISBN 978-1-78623-079-9

Introduction

The question that a lot of people ask is how is it that two people who begin at the same place in life, who go through the same setbacks and difficulties, but when you meet both a decade later, one of them will be successful and the other will not have achieved anything. What decides how two people who go through the same situations achieve very different things in life?

The truth of the matter is that we are in charge of our own destiny, whether we know it or not, and the people who are successful in life know this. We can only be successful in life if we take control of our lives rather than let life control us. People who are successful control their circumstances and they do not allow these circumstances to control them or dictate their potential, they realise that if we fulfil our potential we will get all the things that we want in life. I was bullied in high school and told by some teachers that I would never achieve anything in life. But I had a belief that was stronger than what people were saying; I believed that if I kept working hard I would achieve everything I wanted to achieve in life. You have to believe in yourself and you have to tell yourself that you are better than just good. You can do anything you want to do if you really believe you can achieve what you set your mind to.

One of the things that hampered my belief in myself was listening to what other people were saying: never let other people determine your potential. For so long, I waited for people to tell me what I was good at; if someone said I was good at something, no matter how much I hated it and knew that I would never do it very well, I went ahead and did it anyway. I was a nobody, but I really believed from the bottom of my heart that I was a somebody. That is a very important part of being a successful person, really believing in yourself that you are a somebody even when people say that you will amount to nothing in life. If you really believe that you can then you will.

In this book I am going to show you what makes success and what makes people with great potential to amount to nothing. I will show you the power that your mind has to change your life; or completely destroy your life if you do not use your mind for the purpose that God intended.

If you are losing hope and you think it is time to give up because things will not work out for you: come on the journey with Frank Saliki: a kid who was told he was not good enough to achieve big things in life; the kid who took a really difficult journey to achieve all he has achieved thus far and show the world that anything is possible. This book will show you that being successful is very easy to do if you put your heart and mind to it. I wrote *Arise and Shine* two years ago and it has been on my laptop all this time, this is my journey, this my story, these are my lessons, this is *Arise and Shine*!

Chapter 1

A Vision for the Future

If you were to monitor a group of one hundred young people and see where they end up in their lives by the time they reach 65 years old, you would find that the result would vary greatly. You will also discover that only a low percentage of these people will have achieved very highly in their lives. Earl Knightdale suggested that this figure was as low as five percent. The question is how come, out of one hundred young people who start out with the same plan and good intentions when they are young, end up achieving different things in life? Is the answer that some people were born to be winners and others are born to be losers? This is certainly not true because we are all born to win, we are all born with talents and if we decide to use them we will achieve all our goals.

So back to the question, why do the minority achieve a lot in life and the majority of people just live mediocre lives, trying to convince the whole world that they are happy with what they have achieved, but in reality, they wish they could turn the clock back and try again. The difference is whether someone has a vision or not. Where are you? Where are you going? What do you need to do to get where you want to go? Every great achievement in life and in Business always begins with a vision; a vision that gives you the direction of where you are going. I am going to use a lot of examples from my time in high school to illustrate how we can put this book to work in real life. Remember, everything you are going to read in this book you have probably heard and you have read it somewhere, you probably have it on your desk at work or on your bathroom mirror.

Now back to the point of having visions, I remember walking around the school grounds and feeling different from the rest of the students in my school. It was like all the kids in school belonged on Earth and I had just been dropped from Mars. I remembered sitting there just trying to fit in, the more I tried the more I felt I really did not fit in. We had just moved to Wales, in the United Kingdom, from the small country of the Democratic Republic of Zambia. My English was just about good enough to get by and the biggest struggle of my life was about to start.

I started school in the UK halfway through year 10 and during the second week of me being in the school we had year 10 exams. I have to say it was not the ideal way to fit into the British education system. I had missed half a year; I was playing catch up from the start. Fitting in and catching up on all my subjects was going to be the biggest challenge of my young life (I did not know that at the time). Can I just point out that challenges in life are what make us human and if you know anyone who has achieved great success in their lives and they tell you that the road to success was very easy, the chances are they are probably not telling you the truth. Every successful person will tell you how at one point they almost gave up all together.

I got the dreaded results and they were appalling to say the least. Through taking my exams, I had realised that I had a lot to learn. A lot of people would have looked at this situation and used the excuse that you were in a new school in a new country; you were always going to struggle. Looking back now, this was probably the case, but I beat myself up so much that I felt that I was not good enough. I felt like a failure, I felt that I would never achieve anything in life at all. I felt inferior to the other kids in school. My inferiority complex was born and it was going to take a lot to overcome it. I really believe that I did not deserve the best things that life has to offer. It was going to be a long road to success; I thought success was meant for everyone else but not me. Some teachers told me that I would not achieve anything in life. And you know that kid in the school playground who is walking around on his own with everyone laughing at him and throwing food and drink at him? I was that kid. Suffering from an inferiority complex because of my poor exam results. My self-esteem was being eaten away at a very fast rate. I was starting to feel more and more inadequate as each day went by. So not only was I struggling academically, my school social life was suffering too. All I wanted to do was to hide away from everyone. I remember praying every night: "Oh Lord, my God, why have you forsaken me?" I was hoping it was going to get better soon. I woke up every morning wondering if this was the day that all my troubles were going to be over: wondering if this was the day I was going to get my school career back on track. These hopes were instantly shattered when I walked through the school gate, I had that feeling again. I felt I was not good at anything; I was a waste of space, I would never amount to anything. The determining fact for me is that I absolutely believed that I was not good enough.

After a year of pure struggle, the dreaded year 11 exams were here. I had prepared for them. To be fair, I had been playing catch up throughout the year and never really caught up with the rest of the students. I was behind in every subject apart from Religious Education and Business Studies and my History was not too bad either. However, I was below average in the other subjects. It was the longest two weeks of my life. I was extremely tired by the end of it but I was dreading what was going to come in August. I got the results hoping for a miracle but I did not pass my exams; I had FAILED! I watched all my classmates jubilant with their results as I walked off the school premises with happy voices disappearing away in the distance, wondering what the future held for me. What was I going to do? I was not as special as the rest of the people in my school. The realisation that I would amount to nothing had hit me; I walked home ashamed and embarrassed. I was a failure! I thought of the joy I saw in the parents of my classmates and I then realised I would not see that look in my parents' eyes. That destroyed me; I stopped at a bus stop and cried. I closed my eyes and then opened them again, looking at my results wishing they were different and as I opened my eyes I realised that it had happened and nothing could be changed. Suddenly, a conversation I had with the head of the sixth form just after I opened my results came back into my mind. I was so disappointed that I did not register that conversation,

I was not going to do my A levels but all was not lost. There was an alternative course I could do and it was only offered in Business Studies, which was one of my better subjects. If I was to pass the Course I was going to do my A levels and, in that very moment, I had a new vision;

Suddenly the voices of people telling me that I would never achieve anything in life were gone and a new vision was born. I didn't know it then, but I look back now at that moment as the moment I started a journey to become a successful student, a journey to a happy life. I started a quest to discover what my strengths were rather than focussing on my weakness. I knew what all my weaknesses were, but did not know my strengths. I burst into song out of the blue; it was one of my favourite Sunday School hymns called *Speak Lord We Hear*. The opening line to this hymn is: 'Listen for the voice that softly speaks in the in most heart'. At that moment, there was a voice that was softly speaking inside me. That very moment I decided that no matter how hard it was going to be, I was going to become somebody, I was going to go to university like anyone else. I then decided I may not have made my parents proud but a day would come when I would fill them with joy untold.

And so my second journey began; I took up a Course called BTEC Business Studies. Our class was made up of all the people who had not done well in their exams the previous year. I have to say it was a room full of people with no dreams at all. The class was made up of people who set their bars just too low and hit. The motivational speaker Les Brown once said "people fail in life not because they set their bars too high and miss, people fail because they set their bars too low and hit" My BTEC class was a fitting example of this. Most people in the class had set their bars just too low, as I found out a few years later most of them hit. We were the class that was considered to be the dummies of the school and a lot of people in my class really believed this. But I was different from the rest. I knew what I wanted to do at the end of the year. I knew I was going to do my A levels and go on to university. I did not know how I was going to get there but I knew that, somehow, I was going to get there. That's all I had, a dream.

A lot of people do not succeed in life because they cannot even dare to dream. This fact that a lot of people do not even dare to dream has meant that a lot of them are leading unhappy lives. When I had a vision of going to university, I knew I had limitations and weaknesses, but I also realised that I had abilities that no one else had. I never realised most of my abilities until my third year of university. However, one summer morning in 2007 I had realised that I had something in me and I was going to use it to get the best out of life. The other students who did really well in their exams laughed at me all the time, but I realised that for the first time it didn't bother me. This was because, at the age of 17, I realised that it was *my* life and there was only one person who would determine where I ended up life and that was *me*. The great American writer and broadcaster Earl Nightingale quipped: "We are all self-made but only the successful will admit it."

I had a dream and for a person like me to have a dream a lot of people thought it was far-fetched. I am here to tell you that no matter how far-fetched your dream may seem, if you have a vision you will find your promised land on earth. You will find that place that fills you with great joy and happiness. It all starts with a vision in your heart and mind. During my BTEC year I learnt a lot about myself. I discovered that I am not one to follow the crowd. A lot of people have visions but they are all destroyed because everyone is doing what everyone else is doing. I will talk more about being yourself later.

Why is having a vision so important? I would like you to imagine this: you are enjoying a lovely cruise and you discover that the captain of the cruise ship has got no directions whatsoever and he will just take a chance and see whether he gets you there or not. How many of you would go on that cruise I wonder? I know I wouldn't. So why do you want to live life without a vision or direction? Zig Ziglar, an American author and motivational speaker, believed that the only people who are going to win are those who prepare to win. If we have a vision, we will prepare; if we have no vision, we will not prepare to win because we will not know where we are going.

The BTEC Business Studies course flew by and, before I knew, it was the beginning of the new school year. I had passed my BTEC year and it was time for my A levels. I cannot remember a time in my life I was more excited than I was the first day of my A levels. It was a new beginning and all past failings were forgotten; it was time to look forward. Never waste your valuable time looking at all your past failings when you can look forward and rewrite your life story and move from defeat to victory.

For the first time in my school life I made very close friends who remain so to this day. I became one of the most valuable members of our form group. I saw myself differently hence the whole world saw me differently. To cut a long story short, I had two years of A levels full of pure joy and happiness. I left school with very good results and was accepted in the University of Wales, Newport. But my troubles were not completely behind me and, when I thought I was now settled, depression hit. I had not dealt with all my issues very well and I was feeling it. It was at the end of my first year of university that I realised that I was suffering from depression and I struggled with this battle into my third year of university. I went to my doctor who prescribed tablets, even in the darkest hour I knew that this was not the answer, nor was it going to take me where I wanted to be. The fact that I had a dream and I had a vision helped me to overcome depression and eventually graduate from university. Never ever forget how far you have come and how much you have achieved and keep one thing in your mind: how much you will achieve if you keep going and looking ahead.

One thing that made me go from being a high school failure to a university graduate was my ability to look ahead and not look back. A vast number of people spend most of their lives looking back at what might have been, instead of concentrating on the future and focusing on what could be. Thinking of what might be if you keep moving forward will produce the desired results in life. Yesterday is gone and you will never change it; you do have today to create a better tomorrow. If you are still focussed on what you lost yesterday, the chances are you will miss what today has to bring, hence, in a few years' time; you will still be in the same spot in life. The only people who become successful after going through adversity are those who decide to look ahead and not look at what happened to them in the past. A lot of people look at what happened to them in the past all the time and they end up taking their God given abilities to the grave with them. Oh! to live a life and only to realise that you did not do anything that you were born to do, just because you spent your whole life going over all your failures. If you spend time counting how many times you have tried new things in life and how it had not worked out all the times you tried. This kind of thinking will make you give up on your dreams and on life all together. I failed so many times in my high school years before I started passing any of my exams. When I started getting good results, it was a surprise to everyone, but it was not a surprise to me because I had a vision, I knew where I was going. I knew where I came from but I did not want to look back as it was too painful, and the possibility of the happiness I could find if I carried on striving onwards was too glorious to miss out on.

I imagined myself in a graduation gown with my proud parents standing beside me with big smiles. I imagined standing there with the possibility of a bright future. The idea of achieving all these things sounded better to me than living the rest of my life as a failure. I loved the idea that I would come from the BTEC course, the course considered to be for dummies, and actually achieve my dreams.

This all involved looking forward every day. I did a lot more work than everyone else as well as reading different subjects to help me get a better idea of what subject I was going to do. This was way before I had even passed the BTEC course. Why was I doing this?

This was because I was on a forward-looking journey, I knew what I wanted and I really believed I was going to get there. My big exam failures of the past were not that big anymore; human beings are good at magnifying the smallest setbacks in life and making them bigger than they are. A lot of people actually believe that all the bad things that happen in life were created for them. People will convince you that nothing will ever go right in their lives and they tell you their life story as evidence to show that it is true. They legitimately believe this from the bottom of their hearts. Their belief system tells them that they will not do anything worthwhile in life and that they will not amount to anything in their life because of what happened in the past. What if you just decide to do that one thing that you are really good at? Some school subject perhaps, or is it music that you are truly good at, even when it is not very popular among your age group? What if you decided to do that one thing that you love doing, the thing that truly makes you happy?

Success will only come if you do something that makes you happy. It does not matter how hard it has been or how long the journey to success is going to be: if you really love what you are doing, you are going to enjoy the whole journey. There are a lot of people around today who are not doing anything that makes them happy. They have jobs that they cannot stand only because they do not believe they are good enough to do anything else. I was talking to a woman who has had the same job for 25 years and she told she has hated the job from the first day she walked through the door. I was really puzzled because this was an awful lot of years to be in a place you cannot stand. As I was listening to this woman, I thought what a waste of a life, a lot of years of being unhappy, a lot of years of leaving work and not having that wonderful feeling of a job well done. She told me she wanted to be a designer, but everyone in her family always kept reminding her how many times she had failed in life.

She carried this thought through to her adulthood and she ended up doing something that she was not meant to do. She was not born to work in some government office, she was born to be designer. However, her past experiences and her family told her she was not good enough to be a designer. She listened to what the whole world was saying but she did not listen to the voice that was gently speaking to her, telling her it was possible. I imagine this woman is not the only person out there with a story like this.

Earl Nightingale suggested the number of people doing what they were born to do is very small compared to the number of people who are doing everything in life apart from that one thing that will make them a special talent; that thing that will make all their dreams come true, that one thing that they were born to do. They go to the job they hate every day with these big ideas still burning in their heart and soul, desperate to get used but the past experiences are telling them it is not possible. Their past is saying that other people can live their dreams but not you: you are not special enough.

One thing that a lot of people never realise is that successful people fail on their way to success all the time, the difference is that they learn from all their failures all the time. They see all their failures as a way to make themselves better. They have learnt to look forward at all times and never let the past dictate what they will achieve in the future.

The great Michael Jordan, the legendary NBA basketball player once said, "I missed 6,000 points, lost

300 games and 26 times I was trusted to take the match winning basket and failed." Now Michael Jordan is regarded by most basketball fans as the greatest basketball player of all time. He was exceptionally good at basketball, he still had his flaws but he only concentrated on the things that made him great.

The first time I read Jordan's book I was surprised at the amount of points he missed in his career and how many times he made his team lose a match because he missed a match winning basket. Twenty-six times! For someone as great as him? What about the most significant figure to this, he missed 6,000 points, you what? This is Michael Jordan we are talking about here remember. The same Michael Jordan who is human like you and me. One thing that all human beings have in common is that they all have flaws; they all make mistakes. The difference between Michael Jordan and a lot of people is that he never looked back, he always looked forward. He learnt from his flaws, but the most important factor was that he worked to develop his strength.

He became so good at his strengths that the world never focussed on his weaknesses and failings. If you are to talk to people who have followed this great man's career, you will not find anyone talking about the match that Jordan missed the winning basket only about how great he was. If you stop looking backwards, you will start moving forwards and you will see what is possible for you.

You have to start thinking of things that bring pleasure in your life. A lot of people do not succeed in life because they associate pain with a certain event. One thing that I could not do for a while was to stand in front of people and speak or sing, I associated these two things with great pain. Whenever I spoke in school there was always somebody sniggering in the background. It did not matter whether I was talking about something sensible or not. The reason did not matter, somebody would always laugh. When I was in sixth form this did not bother me anymore, I was looking at the possibilities that were open to me. I convinced myself that if I kept on going, I was going to reach my goal. I had a goal I was aiming at and nothing was going to stop me. I associated looking back with pain and I did not want any more pain; I wanted great pleasure. There was only one way I was going to find that: through looking ahead.

Success will only be achieved by looking forward at all times, the only time you must look back is to look at the lessons you have learnt. I heard somebody say that if they fail five times, they only learn five ways not to do it next time. Remember what I said earlier: do not be afraid of failing. Fail your way to success. Always believe that it is possible and that if other people can do it, so can you. You must always remember that your past does not define you, your future does. Always look ahead to what is to come and not what was or what could have been.

Are you sat there thinking if only I had done this, that or the other, my life could have been different, do you know what you are doing? You are telling yourself that if you do that thing you will be happy, you will be doing what you were born to do and you will win. It is there inside you! Only you are telling yourself the wrong thing. You are telling yourself if this was ten years ago I would do such and such. Well, ten years later, it's about time you start thinking of the next ten years. Imagine what you would become and what your life would be like in the next ten years if you decided to start all over again.

No matter what has happened in the past, it is possible that you can live your dreams. You can do all the things that your talent allows you today. I believe that if a lot of people were to let go of their past experiences they would be very successful. A lot of people today go through life wondering why they are never successful, but the answer is right there in front of them. A lot of people are not successful because they refuse to let go of their past. Their past tells them they are not good enough hence they never look at the possibilities that today and tomorrow brings. A lot of people never realise how many possibilities they miss each day. Every day brings its own possibilities and it is up to us to see these possibilities. We will not be able to see these possibilities if we decide to focus on what happened in the past. God never gave us the power to change the past, however, he gave the great power to change the future. He made us the captains of our souls and the masters of our own destinies. And what a great power to have. This fills me with so much joy because this tells me that I am not a slave to anyone in life, I am responsible for what happens to me. This says I can make my past vanish into thin air. I can create a new world for myself, I can write my own life story. This tells me that other people may have written a story about me losing in life, but if I decide to take charge, I will write a new story. This will be a story in which I am a victor, the story in which I show the entire world that it is possible to win no matter what you have gone through.

However, this can only happen if we realise that we are a work in progress and we take one step at a time. Once we realise that the past will not help us, we should start looking at the possibilities in the future. The problem with a lot of people is that they do the same things that made them fail in life and they expect to get different results. This is not possible. If tomorrow you are doing the same things you are doing today, you are more likely to get the same results. Look at your past and ask yourself this question: are you doing the same thing that made you fail in the past? If that is the case, chances are that you will not succeed. You have to remember that you must always make progress at all times in your life. You must learn new things in your life in order to develop as a person. It is essential that we wake up every morning with a sole purpose of discovering the better you.

You have a sleeping giant inside you and all you need to do is poke it and it will arise. There are a lot of giants out there who have risen but they are not shining at all because they do not know they can be better than what they are, they still let their past tell them they are not good enough. Do not just rise, you must shine as well. Given this thought I decided what was going to be the title of this book *Arise and Shine*. You first arise then shining comes later. However, you must ensure that you are not stuck on arising alone, you must take actions necessary to shine. We are all born to win but a lot of people are chasing the shadows of their past. A lot of people are still mourning all the things they lost in their past when what they need to do is to open their eyes to the possibilities in front of them.

In Anthony Robbins's book, *Awaking the Sleeping Giant*, he says "we all have a giant inside us just waiting to arise and do remarkable things in life" However, I think a lot of us are not aware of the giant that is with us. The giant that will make us do great things in life, the giant that will break down barriers and make a way where there seems to be no way. The giant that is in us will find solutions to problems that most people say there is no solution to. The giant that will tell you that it is possible no matter how hard things are. If we have this giant within us, why are some people doing well whilst other are not? Come on this journey with me and I will show you why. The answer is that those people who are rising and shining have a vision of where they want to be and not a vision of where they were a few years back. Once we have a vision of where we could be, we actively start to find solutions to our problems. We start looking at what we can do to get there and why we are not yet there in the first place.

For a while I was looking for answers to why I was bullied in high School and why some teachers never liked me. Do you want to know where this got me? Absolutely nowhere. I was in the exact same situation. I was stuck where I was. My circumstances only changed once I started looking ahead. I started seeing what everyone around me could not see for me. I started believing that I could be somebody in life and that I could do something worthwhile. I genuinely believed that I was born to win and that everything was possible. You are only going to stand up and start the journey to a successful life if you arise to the possibilities that are around you. You must be aware of all the possibilities around you. Remember, the past is gone and you will never change it even if you try, but you can change your future by deliberately taking action today. Decide where you want to go; no matter how hard it is going to be. Always carry that vision with you; doing this will help you see where you are going. However, this road is not an easy one, the weak will fall by the wayside. The people who always think about what may happen in the future will not get to this promised land called a successful life. Look back at all the things in the past that are holding you back and decide that you will look forward today. The past will cause you a lot of pain, drop it and see the possibilities that the future has for you. Remember we are all self-made, but only the people who have made themselves will really admit it.

The other thing that you must always remind yourself about is that you cannot make it as a wondering generality; you have to become a meaningful specific. A lot of people are walking around without any goals, no goal means you are not aiming at all. You are walking in the dark now. If you do not have a goal and you continue walking in the dark, you will stay where you are in life. However, if you have a goal, you will walk through the dark and step out into the light. If you are walking without a goal in life, you will struggle to find your identity. But once you have a goal, you will go on a discovery journey to find out just how special you are. I believe you were born to win despite your past failures and you must stop looking back and start looking forward. Life can be a struggle but it does not have to be a struggle for the rest of your life. If you understand that it's the struggle in life that gives us strength to deal with the complexities of life, you shall *Arise and Shine*!

Chapter 2

Rise Up to Defeat

It was just another Sunday morning in the valleys of South Wales in the United Kingdom; it was very cold and rainy. My team, Risca Rugby Club under 16s, had a tough rugby match against Blackwood Rugby Club. They really were a tough side, in fact they were the best in our league. It was my first proper rugby match and I was one of the substitutes watching in horror as Blackwood scored try after try. It was really raining tries and every minute it got worse and worse. I came on to make my first Risca appearance when the team was 60 something to 13 down and by the end of the game it was 72–13 to Blackwood. We left the field outplayed, outclassed and defeated; this was not a very good experience. It was embarrassing to say the least. The team had, at this point, played two matches and lost both and we would go on to play eight more games and lose them all; some by huge margins. In our twelfth game against Cwmbran, the elusive win did eventually come, it was a really wonderful feeling. There was joy, relief and pride and for me, unlike the rest of the boys in the team, I enjoyed the feeling of winning a rugby match for the first time. Not only was I on the winning side for the first time in a rugby match it was the first rugby match I played from start to finish. You see, I was not the biggest of guys out there; I am a thin guy so I did not get to start many games.

Why am I telling you this story? Well when the team was doing so badly our coach Jonathan Rowlands did something I thought was unusual for a coach to do when the team was losing. Jon never shouted. In fact, Jon never swore, which is very unusual for a rugby coach today, who are known to swear to get a message across. But not Mr Rowlands. Jon and our backs coach always used to come in with these little pieces of paper. There you would find your rating on the match; it would spell out what you did well and what you needed to improve on. They never criticised us but they told us where we needed to improve which worked well because once we started winning there was no stopping us. We won game after game. I remember sitting there and thinking about how we lost our first eleven but we won the eleven after that. We were not doing badly in the cup either — we got to the semi-finals. I remember this game with very fond memories as in this game I made a 90-metre run just getting tackled a metre or so from the line. Unbelievably we had made it to the final and we faced Blackwood to whom we lost. This was the third time we had played them and we did not win a single game against them.

The truth is I was never going to be a professional rugby player, but I learnt something through this experience. Jon Rowlands taught me that no matter how badly things seem to be if you keep looking for the positives, things will get better. When things are not going very well, a lot of people have a tendency of looking at themselves and thinking they are not good enough. The minute you start thinking that you are not good enough, you will be putting the power of defeat in your mind. Once you have the power of defeat in your mind you will start thinking nothing is possible. Zig Ziglar once said you must fail your way to success. My rugby team and I did this, after losing a lot of matches we eventually got it right by doing the things that we were good at. Mr Rowlands produced a winning team by encouraging each member of the team to use their strengths. This helped the team because everyone felt that they had good abilities and if they maximised these abilities, the team would start winning matches. We should take something from this example. If we focus on the things that we are good at and aim to maximise these abilities we will get the results that we want. We might fail now and again but if we are wise, we will know that there is always tomorrow to try again. For eleven matches, all we did was try and try and again. To be successful all you have to do is try and try again and once we won a game we then made winning a habit. If things are not going as well as you would hope for them to be, never give up and never focus on the negatives. The fact that Jon did not focus on the negatives meant that we as a team remained focused and assured that we were going to win eventually.

Many people spend a lot of time looking at all the things that have gone wrong in their lives and they look at all this and decide success was not meant for them; they make up their minds that they will not achieve anything. The moment we decide that we are not good enough and we will not amount to anything in life, everything that we do will reflect that; a lot of people don't realise that defeat begins in the mind. We were not winning games but Jon knew that he had a group of winners and all he needed to do was to make them believe they were capable of winning. A lot of us manage to convince ourselves that we are not capable of doing anything in life, we truly believe that we were not born to win. Not only do we believe that we were not born to win, we are truly convinced by the fact.

We see a lot of successful people and we say they are different from us, we say they were lucky or grew up in a richer household. However, we don't realise that a lot of successful people might have been through the worst possible experiences that you can imagine. However, they believed that they deserved the best things and never gave up on their quest to reach their destiny. All the success stories you will ever hear happened because those people who are successful did not just sit down and complain when the going was too tough, instead they got tougher.

When we find that things are not going well, we need to look at the strategy that we used in the first place. When I failed my exams, the first thing I had to do was change my learning strategy. You see we all learn differently: some people are brilliant visual learners and others are good audio learners. To be successful in anything in life we have to find a strategy that works for us. A large number of people fail and they attempt to repeat the task in exactly the same manner as they did the first time round. No matter how talented and motivated you are, if you use the same strategy that you used when you were not successful, you will not become successful. However, do not get bogged down on the things that you did wrong, a lot of people fall into this trap and end up feeling even more defeated. A lot of people fail in life not because they did something particularly wrong, but because they did not do the thing that they are good at very well. So next time you attempt anything in your life ask yourself this question: what am I good at? And if you find the answer to that question, ask yourself another question: do I do enough of it?

A lot of us go through life making good attempts at certain things, but we never do enough work on the things that we are good at. Most of the time we don't do something because other people have told us that we are not good enough and we believe that we are not good enough. No matter how many times we have failed, look at and think of the times you did not use the greatest assets you possess: you will not *Arise and Shine* if you keep these abilities to yourself. It's time you came out of your closet and electrify the whole world because there is greatness within you! This greatness has not been manifested only because you have not told yourself you are great enough. You have looked at your abilities and decided you cannot do that because you are not great.

Zig Ziglar once said that you do not have to be great to start, you have to start to be great. No matter how badly you have done in the past, if you decide to pick up the pieces and start over again, you will get what you want in life. A lot of people are too discouraged to even realise that a second chance has been given to them. I worked in a nursing home when I was doing my A levels and having a conversation with a 80-year-old resident made me realise that we get more chances in life than we think. She told me in one of our conversations: "I probably had more than twenty chances in life to be really successful and lead a happy life but I missed them all because I did not have a winning strategy." Sadly I think this a very true for so many people out there; they are not successful because they do not have a winning strategy.

Dr Norman Vincent Pearl in his book *The Power of Positive Thinking* says, "...the only way a man can ever get successful is if they have a strategy." Why a strategy? You must have strategy in your life for everything. You must have a strategy for when things are not going well and when things are going well. A lot of people's strategy for when things are not going well is to complain and blame other people for their circumstances. If you are using this strategy you might as well go out and shout to the world: "I am defeated." Listen, no one likes working with people who blame anyone but themselves when things are not going well.

At some point in life we are going to get things wrong, we are going to be trusted to do a task and we will fail. We are going to be trusted to give a pitch that will secure the business a very good deal and we will fail. Unfortunately, a lot of people will come out from these experiences feeling defeated and for a lot of people these experiences might be life-changing events and not for the better. I remember going for an interview and I left feeling that if I got a phone call back to tell me that I got the job, I would be really surprised. I was on the train home thinking that—barring a divine intervention— there was no way I had the job. You might be reading this and thinking that is a defeated man's thoughts. You see, I had not prepared very well for the interview and therefore did not do very well. I did not hear anything for five whole days and I assumed I had not got the job. I was not defeated I knew that I had not prepared adequately and all I could do was apply for different jobs and just hope for another interview. I went home and applied for more jobs; I got another interview. I decided to change my strategy for this next interview, I decided I was going to be ready for anything, I was going to be ready for any question and I was going to have a lot of good questions to ask. I did not use the negative strategy a lot of people use after an unsuccessful interview, which is to say I am not good enough, I will never get another job. However, I told myself I was good enough for that job, I just never prepared to succeed. In the end, I got the job.

The late great Zig Ziglar once said that "in order to succeed you have to prepare to succeed", however, a lot of people don't do this. People make a lot of plans about their future and they never take into consideration the number of obstacles they will face. A lot of people have a plan of where they want to be, but they do not take into consideration all the ups and downs in the journey to reach where they want to be. You have to ask yourself each and every day whether you are preparing yourself to win or not. You have to ask whether you are doing the one thing each day that will take you closer to your goal or not. A lot of people will tell you what they want in life but they really do not believe that they will achieve it.

For you to start preparing for winning you have to really believe that you are born to win and you can do everything that your talent allows you to do. This means that you really have to sit down and make a list of what you are really good at and what you should focus on. A lot of people go through their lives without thinking of what they are good at instead spending all their lives looking at all the things they are not good at and this list grows massively and they feel super inadequate. What we don't realise is that there is a line between working on weaknesses and eating away at your confidence. We all have our flaws, but if you decide to look at flaws all the time, you will find plenty of them. My advice to you is to start looking at more positives in yourself; focus on all the good things that you have done, even in failure.

I always analyse what I do during the week. I spend a few minutes looking at all the things that I did wrong then I go in for the kill for the good things I did. I do this because when I began the journey from a high school failure to a university graduate, I had to really underestimate my flaws and overestimate my positives. I hear someone say, "Hey Frank, but we can only get better if we really deal with our flaws." My response to that is that our strengths will always be stronger than our weaknesses. A lot of people spend a lot of time working on their weaknesses and they end up finding plenty hence they are not happy with themselves. On the other hand, if people focus on what they are really good at, they will be more positive in their thinking all the time. This does not mean they don't have flaws but this just means that they spend more time developing the skills that will be more useful to them in the long run.

Imagine this situation. A student who is destined to be an accountant is bogged down because he is not very good at art. He spends a lot of time trying to be very good at art and ends up not being very good at it because it is not his calling. Oh, and in the process of doing this what happens to his brilliant maths skills? He loses it and decides he is not good at maths either. This happened because the student did not just focus on the subject he was naturally good at and instead focussed on a subject that he had no chance of winning at. To be successful you have to focus on things that you are really good at. Why do you want to put yourself at the bottom of the art class when you could easily be at the top of the maths or music class? Why are you focusing on the things that you are not good at rather than focusing on the things that you are good at? Wouldn't it be easy then to just focus on those things rather than the weaknesses that might not even be our calling in life?

The answer to this question is that man is too much of a conformist; he always tries to ensure that he fits in with everyone. Trying to fit in has meant that a lot of people have given up on their dreams. Today's society has transformed us into thinking that if you are different from everyone else then there is something wrong with you. It is this feeling of being different that stops a lot of people doing what they really want to do. People will do what other people want them to do or what they think will please others. A lot of people are consumed with the whole idea of being popular, so much so they forget about their dreams. People today seem to think that they must do what other people want them to do and if they do not succeed in that then they are a failure. The reason there are fewer people who are incredibly successful and truly happy in life compared to the people who are not happy and are not doing anything that makes them happy is because very few people are willing to stand up for what they believe in.

A large number of people are living their lives with other people's permission. If you have a dream and you know and truly believe that it will work no matter what, Some people who are close to you may say it can not be done. You know why other people do not believe you can do it? It is your dream and not theirs. No matter how far-fetched it might seem to be, you can only succeed if you really think you can. Oh, and you can only achieve something if you do what you really want to. Our wonderful friend who did a job she hated all her life just because she listened to what her family said and did not look at what talents she had, she only heard what people said. This human desire for approval at all times has cost a lot of people a lifetime of true bliss and happiness.

Before you start looking for approval from other people I want you to remember that true happiness is not found in other people but true happiness is found within. This statement tells us we are only going to be truly happy if we do what we want to. Remember: we were all born to win but we can only win if you do what you were born to do. Winners do not always have people cheering them on when they start but they have a lot of people cheering when they win. You do not have to be like everyone else; you were born to be you. A lot of times if you are different, people will just think you are strange. I remember my time during the last few months of school when we were all choosing our universities. Many people were choosing universities not based on their reputation or the course they wished to study to give them the future they wanted, instead they chose universities because their close friends were going there. What I found ironic about all this is that when I met some of these people a couple years later they were not friends anymore.

Every single day people make decisions that will shape their lives forever, but they are more focussed on who agrees with their decision. If you are depending on other people to tell you whether you are good enough then you are already defeated. You have to own your own life; it is yours and no one else's. I am not saying that you should not listen to advice but we all know people who will constantly tell us it cannot be done, or someone else will tell you that you are not great. First of all, you can if you think you can; if other people can do it you can do it. You do not have to be great to start, you have to start to be great!

You have to remind yourself that you may be the only one walking this road but you don't care because this was the road that was laid for you and no one else. It may look like you are going in the wrong direction but this is where your destiny is. Your road to success is laid out for you, but next to the road of success there is road of failure. It looks easier because you don't have to work really hard to stay on that road, in fact you don't do anything to stay on that road where life is very easy. Whereas, those who are working on their dreams find a lot of obstacles in their way. They have to deal with people telling them they will never make it. However, in the end, the person who is working on their dreams will lead a happy life, unlike the person who followed what people without dreams told them to do. It is your dream and it is your life to take charge of and don't let other people determine what you can do. People who are successful in most cases choose to be successful and those who are failures choose to be failures.

Now that last statement may sound very harsh but that is the whole truth. We are all self-made but only the successful will admit it. We are what we are today because that's all we want to be. Life is made up of all the choices that we have made in the past and the choices we are going to make today and in the future. This seems just so simple: is life really just made of our choices? A resounding yes. We can choose to stop following the crowd and do what we really want to do or we can continue to follow the crowd. We can get up today and do what we have been putting off for days, weeks, months or even years and start today, or we can put it off and stay where we are. You can be whatever you want to be, only if you really want to. Thinking about this point makes me sad, the fact the we have got a choice to be what we want to be and we can be what we really want to be, but only if we really want to when a lot of people just blame other people for their failures.

It makes me think of our friend who would have been a fashion designer if she had really wanted to. At this point I will talk about one of the most important institutions in our society today and that is family. When we set goals in life a lot of us want to make our family happy for us. When I failed my exams, my biggest and deepest desire was to make my parents proud of me and that was it. However, as the months went on I realised that this was not about my parents, this was about me doing what I want to do. I started dreaming of having a better, brighter future. I started thinking of building a brighter and better me.

At different points in my journey my parents told me what I was really good at and what I was not good I remember one sunny March morning in 2008. My dad brought his friend to come and talk to me about changing my studies. He suggested that I should do a different subject and my dad supported him. There was only one problem: I had no interest whatsoever in what he was suggesting to me. In fact, at this point I had already decided I was going to do a business degree at university. This was two and half years before I went to university. I could have changed all my plans but I knew where I was going and what was waiting for me. I could visualise it in my mind and managed to feel the joy within myself that was to come and I told myself all the time I was going to make it no matter how hard it was or was going to be, nothing would stop me.

Understanding that we are all unique and that we can be born with talents which our parents do not possess is very important. A lot of people spend their lives trying to be like their parents, therefore they do not use the talents that they are born with. Parents are the most important people in our lives, they care for us and they watch us grow up, however, some parents want to hold on to their little boy or little girl forever. They want to stay in control of their children and will stop at nothing to ensure that their child will come back to them for everything. This stops the child from growing and venturing into new waters. This results in the child doing the bare minimum and setting their bar too low and they hit it. Success is a progressive realisation of worthy goals as we discussed earlier. If your parents have so much control over your life, you spend the rest of your life trying to be your parents and not yourself.

Our parents are very important; they bring us up and provide for us. I consider myself to be fortunate to have had a very caring mother. I remember growing up in the small mining town of Luanshya in the northern part of Zambia and how wonderful things were until the company that owned the mines left. The majority of people in this town worked in the mines and when the mine closed the result was very detrimental to the whole town. This is the time I saw my mother's love of work. She continued working at the local hospital without pay for up to six months at a time. My mother always managed to provide for us. The most we ever went without food was having one good meal a day. This meant that unlike other children in a similar situation, my brother and I were able to perform well in school. In the words of Les Brown "...for who I am and what I am I owe it to mother," and I really do owe it to my mother. It's only now that I realise what she did: she taught me that no matter how bad things may be at the moment, they will get better. For all she did and all she does and for all she will do, I will always have great respect and love for my mother. However, I will never let my mother stop me from living my dream. A lot of young people think their parents know them better than they know themselves. But the reality is that there is no human being in the world who will know you better than you know yourself. A lot of young people are not doing what they were born to do because they are always seeking their family's approval in everything that they do. They have a burning desire to do a lot better in life, but they are doing what their family wants them to do and not what they want to do.

The wonderful thing about life is that you can do everything that your talents allow you to do, only if you want to. Our parents love us but remember that if they grew up being told they would not achieve something because it is beyond them, they will tell you the same. Do not be defeated just because your parents tell you it is impossible. What I have learnt in life is that a lot of people have been told a lot of times it is not possible and they pass this on to their children. Many people think that just because something has not been done before then it will never be done. Growing up in Africa, I found people who believed that success and failure truly depended on whether your family are successful or not. However, success is for everybody. It is the realisation of worthy ideals. The realisation that everything is possible and that if you can dream you can do it will change your life. Listen, if other people did not see it for themselves, there would be no chance on earth they will see greatness for you. Have you ever asked your parents if they studied hard, worked hard, did more than they were paid to do, and never gave up when the going got tough? The chances are they probably did not do this, they probably gave up easily and the chances are that if you were to make it, they would be there singing your praises. So, although your parents may criticise you for a short period of time for following your dream, they will surely sing your praises forever when you make it. As long what you are doing will not harm your family, go for it. Even though they are against your decision at the time, do not be defeated because you will only *Arise and Shine* if you do what you were really born to do.

The fact that something has never been done before is not a reason for not doing it. All the technology that we use today had to be developed by someone! When you have a great idea, work at it even though you might not be doing very well. When this happens, people close to you might tell you that they were right, that they knew that your dream was not going to turn into a reality. This is a very important stage of any successful life. The people who are able to get passed this stage become successful in whatever they are doing.

Certain people are failures in life because they have never tried anything difficult or they gave up when the going got tough. Do not be deflated because something is going slower than you expected. You have to be really patient with yourself. You have that talent therefore you are the only one who can do that. The fact that today is not going well does not mean that tomorrow won't be any better. Maybe tomorrow will not be any better or even the day after, but if you keep going, you will find what you are looking for one day. The day will come when you reach that Promised Land as long as you do not give up on that dream. The dream you are carrying now, only you can make it possible. What is the point of not doing the things you really want to do when you are not going to leave this world alive anyway? It will get hard. In my journey to go to university there were times when I thought, is it worth it? And the answer was yes. Was it necessary that I went to university? Was it imperative that I never gave up? And the answer was yes. I then asked myself if there was anything else I wanted to do apart from going to University and the answer was nothing else. After answering these questions, I knew I could not afford to give up on my dream, even though I was not really sure I was going to achieve it.

Make up your mind about what you want to do. Do not focus on the 'how' part because it will come later on in the journey; focus on the 'why' you have to do it. I did what I did because I wanted to have a job and earn a living after; I did what I did because I knew that if I achieved my goal I would find true bliss and happiness and then the 'how' followed later in the journey. Life is a journey and the more we move forward the clearer the view will become. You may not see the fruits of your labour today but—believe me—when you keep watering and fertilising them you will soon see the result. Sometimes progress is not noticed by the person until later on when they discover that they are able to do something they thought they could not do. When you start working on your dream there are a lot of things you will not know, but when you start working, all these things will become clear and you will start to get the answer to the 'how' question. Always remember this: the 'how' will come one day. All you have to do is keep going because if you give up, the 'how' will definitely elude you forever. I believe that there are very few successful people in life because few people are looking beyond their failures. On your journey to your dream, you will encounter setbacks and people will tell you it cannot be done and others will tell you that your face does not fit.

As long as you believe it is possible, one day all those people who laughed at you on your journey to success will sing your praises. Those are the people who did not really want to be around you, those who said, "He is mad he will never do anything." One day on the train from work, a guy I knew from school came and sat next me and he started chatting to me. I did not realise who it was until 15 minutes into journey, he was one of the kids who bullied me in school! He was one of the people who thought I was nothing and now he sat there singing my praises and marvelling at the fact that I was doing well for myself. Just because people tell you are not good enough to achieve something that does not mean you should throw in the towel. If you want to start something and you think that you are not good enough always carry this quote with you: "You do not have to be great to start, you have to start to be great."

The determining factor of your successes is you and not your circumstances. It is you, and it is always going to be you, who is going to determine where you end up tomorrow and in ten years' time. Always try to do what other people won't do today so you can have things other people won't have tomorrow.

However, I would like to remind you that certain events are sometimes going to happen that we will have no control over. I remember when the 2008 global financial crisis happened, a lot of people lost their jobs and some of whom had held their jobs for years or even decades. They did not have much control of what was going on in the global economy, however, they had a choice to sit out or to join in. Sit in or sit out, what am I on about? They had a choice to say that all they had worked for all their lives was gone and they would never get it back, or they could have gone on a mission to get it all back.

Here is an example. Two people lose their jobs and one decides they will do anything that they can to find another job. The economy is so bad they cannot find employment anywhere but continue looking. They refuse to listen to people who are defeated and never stop until they find something. On the other hand, the second person has faced rejection after rejection and has given up and is spending time with friends who have also given up. Spending all day watching television just to see to how bad things are out there. Fast forward five years later, the economy has picked up, the person who never gave up has a very good job and has managed to work themselves into a better position than in their previous job. Now we can guess what happened to the other person who has spent the last seven years convincing themselves that there is no hope and has become very argumentative.. Good heavens! How depressing was that! Well that is how life works: you get what you put in. The second person defeated themselves by looking at the negatives of the time but never thought of the future that might be brighter than today.

I remember the day that I failed my exams a dream was born; I was knocked down but I did not get knocked out. It was a major setback in my life, however, I refused to sit on the side lines of my own life. The day that a lot of people would be defeated, a giant in me was born. I was ready for battle for the first time in my life. I was going face everything that was to come my way; I was young, ready and hungry. The journey to that graduation stage was long and hard, I faced setback after setback. Although I suffered with depression most of my second year of university, I had a dream and I was going to make it happen. I threw away the tablets because I did not need them, all I needed was to keep going and not stop until I was done. I was ready to face life head on and I understood that I would face setbacks in the future, but it would not be over until I reach that Promised Land called success. I refused to dwell on my past failures because I knew that I would never change the past but I could change tomorrow. I believed that if I constantly did something to make me grow, I would make it. I refused to overestimate my weaknesses and underestimated my strength. Winners always know that if they keep going, they will achieve their goals. Remember a boxing match is only over when the opponent stays down;, you may get knocked down but whatever you do not get knocked out. No matter how hard things are make sure that you stay in the game of life. You can change your life if you think you can. If you are not happy about where you are, you can change it.

Sometimes we will do everything possible to succeed in life and certain circumstances will change the course of our life. My very close friend in university had plans to be a teacher and after we finished university she went back for another year so that she could embark on a teaching career. She was going to have another year at university and she was going to be a qualified teacher; good plan. My friend was a single parent at this point, she went through university being a single mum and sometimes she did not make lectures because she couldn't find anyone to look after her little one. When we were talking after we had finished university, I found out that we both suffered depression at the same time. She had had a long journey to get here as well and she thought she found what she wanted to do. In the first few months of her teacher training, she had a fit and she was not allowed to drive and had to give up her teaching career before she had even started. She had a mortgage to pay and a child to feed and clothe, she thought she would have to sell her house. She never became defeated, instead she started trying to find out what else she could do. Well, she just did a business degree so you know what she decided? She was going into business. She had never run her own business but she was determined to make it a success. She is a parent so all she had to do was to look at what children like, and so 'Little Hands Play' was born. She only started it off as an online store in the middle of 2014, but, by the beginning of 2015, she had her own little shop in her local area. I can never recall a day of her complaining about what was going wrong in her life; she wanted to be successful and that was it. Don't be defeated because your best plans have gone astray, there is always going to be something in life.

I believe that sometimes life will force you to do what you were really born to do even if you are not already doing it. Life will pass you by very quickly if you spend all your life feeling sorry for yourself: stand up and take a leap of faith. I think my friend Libby decided she was going to see by faith and not by sight. Do not focus on what you are seeing right now, believe that it is possible for you no matter how hard things may be at the moment; it is possible for you to eventually achieve your dream.

In the time my friend was deciding what she was going to do next, my dream of going to university was not going well either. After I had left university, I applied for over three hundred jobs and I probably had less than five responses. It was a very difficult time for a graduate; the economy was just recovering and this meant that we were competing for jobs with very experienced people who had lost their jobs during the recession and I knew it was going to be a very long road. I remember when I got my first interview, it was exciting. I was going to get this one I told myself, and I got it. It was a job in a HR department and I had just done a degree in business and human resources, dream come true. It was a three-month contract and I was going to do everything possible to make them keep me longer than the three months the job was contracted for. I worked exceptionally hard, I was in work earlier than was expected and leaving later than expected. I was doing everything possible to show the management that I was a good worker. It was going well, I was loving it; I thought to myself this is what I went to university for. By the time we got to the second week, I was thinking that I was working myself into a longer contact. I started dreaming of having long-term goals in this job and one morning all this was shattered. My manager called me into their office and said they did not have any work for me anymore. I had so much enthusiasm about this job, and, in what felt like a twinkling of an eye, it was all taken away.

I was happy to have this job and I did the best I could have done, the lesson I learnt from this experience is that sometimes we will do the best we can but things will still not work out. We then have a choice to keep holding on to the project that has failed or move on to the next one. I refused to keep holding on to what could have been and I went after what will be. I received a lot of rejections on the way but I was determined I was going to find something. Sometimes all you need to do is keep knocking and knocking. I had rejection after rejection so I knocked on door after door. After about another hundred job applications, I found a job. We have a key in our hands and there is a door out there that it will open if we keep trying. Sometimes we will have to confront over a hundred doors before one opens.

You have to remember that everything that is worthwhile does not come easy; it is worked and sweated for. The only people who reach the Promised Land called success are those who refuse to be defeated, no matter what they have gone through. I can remember going through a lot of interviews and thinking to myself that the right one will come. When I received all rejections, all I did was apply for another job. You were born to live your dream so, no matter how bad things are or are going to be, tell yourself you are not just going to settle for anything, you are going to do what you were born to do. Life is not a sprint, it is marathon and he who endures to the last will find the glory that he is looking for.

The fact of life is that hard times will fall on all of us and not a selected few. The difference is that very few people believe they can turn their lives around when things are not going well, you have to really believe that it is possible. You must understand that sometimes you will have to fail your way to success, sometimes you will do everything necessary to succeed at something and it will simply not work out. You then have to make a decision: either you are going to sit out the rest of your life or you are going to play an active role in your life. This is how life works, you will have setbacks but, whatever you do, do not sit out the rest of your life. Remember this: you might fail today, but you have tomorrow to start all over again. The day I failed my exams a dream was born, why? Because I knew that I had been putting myself down because other people were putting me down and I was determined. My confidence did not improve overnight, I built it up as I went on this long, unknown journey to get to university. Remember that setbacks are part of life; in my failures I learnt to remain strong and determined. We will fall short now and again but if we get knocked down and we get up, we will *Arise and Shine*!

Chapter 3

It's You!

The reality of life is that we are going to face a lot of trials and tribulations along the way and it's up to us to rise up to these challenges. The only people that will succeed in life are those who face the challenges of life head on. We have the power to do great things in life but most of us are hiding this away all the time. I truly believe that if we all stepped out of our comfort zones, we would achieve great things in life.

In this chapter, I will talk about having control of our lives and I will show you how I took back control of my own life. I went from a high school failure to a university graduate in six years because I did not want to be failure for the rest of my life. The biggest question you must ask yourself is, do you want to be where you are now? Who can change the current circumstances you find yourself in right now?

The great Earl Nightingale in his famous speech, *The Strangest Secret*, said, "...we are all self-made but only the successful will admit it." He refutes the whole idea that we are all shaped by our circumstances or wealth, but he argues that we are all self-made. He goes on to say that we determine where we end up in life and not other people. I agree with his view entirely: we are truly self-made. Why do I agree with him? Well, when I failed my high school exams I could have looked at all the things that went wrong in my high school life leading up to the exams. You know what would have happened? I could have spent another three years feeling sorry myself and ended up in a job I did not like. What I did that August morning was to take charge of my life. I knew that there was only one way I was going to be successful. I hated the thought of being an adult and going to a job I did not like. I thought to myself that God did not put me on this earth to be a failure. In all my time in high school I never thought I would ever amount to anything, but on the day that I failed my exams I believed I could amount to something. However, only if I decided to put my running shoes on and join the marathon called life. The only way you can ever win a race is if you finish. The great thing about the race called life is that it has a lot of winners and all they have to do is finish. We have very few people who are successful today because a lot of people have stopped halfway through because it has got too hard.

No one should decide whether you should stop or continue: you have the power to control this. I talked in the previous chapter how family influences our decisions in life. People will tell us it cannot be done or you will never do that, but the final decision is in our hands. We make that decision whether we will continue or not. Remember that people are going to have their opinions about our dream, but if we have conviction about our dream, nothing will stop us. I believe that a lot of people give up on their dreams because they are not convinced enough.

Follow your dream even if people around you are not doing it or even if it's never been done before. Remember you are better than good and you can do anything you want to do, but only if you think you can. I believe successful people know that they have the power to get where they want to go. They believe that the only thing that determines whether they make it or not are themselves. They do not waste time looking at the situation in the economy or other global events to determine whether they should do what they want to do. The truth is we determine our own success and not environmental circumstances. As a Christian, I have always believed that I should do what I can and God will take care of all the things I cannot do; you have to do what you can do and the rest will take care of itself. Never lose the faith because that's the only thing that will keep you on track. You have to do things that give you strength, and if you notice that what you are doing now is not what you really want to do, no matter how far away you maybe from your desired road, there is still time to turn around now.

I think human beings underestimate the power that they have over every situation they face in life. Read Dr Norman Vincent Pearl's book *You Can If You Think You Can* and see how many times he says you can if you think you can. This means that you can do something only if you think you can. When I made up my mind to go to university after failing my exams, I did not know how I was going to get there, all I knew was I was going to get there. However, I did not sit back; I had to take action to achieve my goal. I had to make sure that I worked out what worked better for me. No one had to sit me down and tell me what works best for me, I made that decision myself.

Sometimes we look for answers for success in the wrong places, most of the times the answers we go searching for from everyone else are only found within. We have most things we need inside us, but we just don't use these things. I spent the whole BTEC year trying to work out what was the best learning strategy for me. Guess what? I found it, I found what works for me and what doesn't. I discovered what I was really good at and I stuck to it. Once I discovered it, I really did perform in school, my results rose dramatically, and my dream of going to university was well and truly on. It was not a sprint at this point, but it was a fast jog at least. I remember telling myself that I was on course and the dream is underway. To a lot of people, I was still this kid who had failed his high school exam, but that that kid was no more; the kid was seeing possibilities for himself.

Failing my exam was really painful, I can still feel the pain and anguish I had that sunny August morning and I refused to feel so much pain ever again. My circumstances did not matter anymore. I got tired of being this bullied kid in school; I got tired of being the kid everyone laughed at all the time; I got tired of being a failure. That day I refused to go for lesser things in life, but I decided to go for things that will bring pure joy, I was going to live my dream. My advice to you today is that if you want to be truly successful and happy you have to leave all the things that bring pain to your life behind; if you are still holding on to things, this will only bring pain in your life. Up to the time I left school, some teachers never really believed that I could amount to anything. However, I had built myself up for three years and I was going to make it no matter how hard the road was going to be. You have to have passion for what you want to achieve. I dreamt of going to university all the time; it was the last thing I thought of before bed and the first thing in the morning. I was ready and hungry I believed that my time to *Arise and Shine* was around the corner.

I wanted this so much that if I had to run through a wall—although I would probably have not succeeded—I promise I would have tried a few times. I had a dream and I believed I could turn it into a reality. That dream you are holding inside you today is waiting to be manifested and the only person who can do that is you; it's time to *Arise and Shine* and do what you were born to do.

You have to start creating a better you today, try and be the best you can, tell yourself you can be better than good. You have to believe you can do better and take action. You have to start by taking that first step. You have to look at your work and everything you do and ask yourself: do I put 100% into everything that I do? Do you do just about enough to not get fired? A lot of us when we go to work will think we are doing our boss a favour, which is not true. If we decide we are going to do the minimum work we are not hurting our boss, we are hurting ourselves. We are stopping ourselves from climbing that ladder. You do not have to listen to other people about how you should do your job, you have to decide to make a difference and sometimes that may involve you working for more than what you are paid for. I hear someone say how on earth does that benefit you? Well the benefits are huge. First of all, you might not know it, but your superiors are watching the work you are doing and when an opportunity comes up for a promotion they will look at your work ethic and they will say: 'that's the man or woman for the job.'

Have you ever noticed that the people who always tell you not to work very hard have been in the same job for many years and they do not like it? They do just about enough to not get fired and when a new employee comes in they try and give the self-same advice that has made them be mediocre. You have to be careful with the source of your advice; you don't want to lessen your talent just because you listened to the wrong crowd.

The disappointment of having my contract cut short could have made me give up all together, what was the point of going through what I went through to get there and then having it all taken away? I refused to give away the power of living a successful life to somebody else. You have to stay in control of your life and the only way you will ever stay in control is by having the knowledge that we are self-made and that we can change our lives no matter what we have gone through. Some people have grown up in very rich families and they have all the advantages in life and they have not made it. On the other hand, you have all at some point heard great stories of people who came from total poverty to great success. The people who had to work very long hours to get where they are today. These are the people who refused to accept the idea that they will never achieve anything in life. You do not have to settle where you are; you have to stop looking at what you are not good at and focus on the things you are really good at.. You have your own talents and it's up to you to find them. Don't spend every day of your life trying to see if you can be better than your friends; you simply have to try and become a better person than you were yesterday. You have to develop your skills each day of your life. You have to look at your job and see what you need to develop. If you say you don't have any flaws in your work, you are only cheating yourself. You have to really work on what you are good at and if a weakness is making you fall short of your dream, you have to really work on it. No one else will do this, only you can do it; you have to protect the dream like you would a baby.

You will get other people who will tell you it cannot be done, but as long you believe it can be done, it will be done. I can remember the feeling in the last semester of university. There were three months to go to my last exam and 'Frank can do this' turned into 'Frank will do this!' So many times on my journey people told me I would not be able to make it and some people said they would put their mortgage on me not making it out of university. It was not about what people thought that mattered, it was what I thought that was the determining factor of my success. I really wanted to make it and I was going to make it because I thought I could and I thought I deserved it. You see my friends: a quitter never wins and a winner never quits. You should never stop until you are done; you have to do what you have to do and the rest will take care of itself. A lot of people never play their part in life and things don't work out for them. You have to be ready for an opportunity even if you have not got one. Les Brown once said, "It is better to be ready for an opportunity and not have one than to have an opportunity and not be ready for it." You have to be ready for opportunities at all times.

In chapter two I talked about missing out on a job because I did not prepare for the interview, well from this experience I learnt that if I fail to prepare, all I am doing is preparing to fail. I believe that a lot of people are doing this each and every day. If you were to ask a lot of people what they want to do in the next five years, I assure you a lot of people would not give you a definite answer.

A large number of people have let other people talk them out of their dream because they want to please other people. These days a lot of young people are easily influenced by other people and their friends. You have to make sure that the people you are spending a lot of your time with are building you up and not putting you down. Ziglar in one of his seminars said: "We are all where and what we are because of what goes in our minds." We must be careful who gives advice and whom we spend time with. In my first months in high school I spent time with people who did not want me around them and they told me all the things I was not good at. Whenever I gave a wrong answer on the few occasions I raised my hand, there was always someone laughing. You see I did not have to spend any time with these people; all I was doing was trying to get their approval and the only thing I needed was to accept myself for who I am. You might be the nicest person alive, but, believe me, there is always going to be someone who does not like you. A lot of us are here because of what other people have told us and not what we have told ourselves. You are the master of your own destiny and not the world; no one else will create a better you than you.

You have to have a good idea of where you are going, you will not get anywhere in life if you do not have a clear plan of where you want to go. A sailor has a clear plan of where he wants to go even though he does not see the destination until the very last of the journey. I was talking to my friend one day and he said to me that he didn't like making goals because things change in life very quickly. That is the whole idea of having short term goals within your main goal. Short term goals deal with the changes, they give you time to adjust and stay on course. You will never get ahead in life if you do not have a goal. Remember that success is a worthy realisation of worthy goals and if you do not have a goal to work for, you will not be successful in life. After all, you cannot be successful at doing nothing. How can you expect to be successful in life by doing nothing at all? You have to take actions towards your goal and you are the only one who can take those actions. Whatever you do, never let other people talk you out of your dreams. When I made up my mind I was going to university, I was going to university and no one was going to stop me. If you have a dream you have to be convicted because a lot of people might try to talk you out of it; be who you want to be and not what other people want you to be. You were born to win and you can, only if you think you can.

A lot of people live life without following their own directions; you have to have your own direction because you are the only the person who can make the dream you have a reality. A lot of people do not have any direction in their lives whatsoever. They just follow what other people tell them and without thinking they follow. I saw this view in action when Mrs Thatcher passed away during my last year of university. When she was British Prime Minister she oversaw the closures of the coal mines in the UK. When she passed away all the former mining towns had big parties, people in these areas were happy because the person who apparently ruined their lives was dead. The first thought that came to mind when all this was going on was, how can a man sink so low just to justify his own failures in life? Some of these people who were celebrating had not even been born when the mines closed. They refused to leave the areas where there are no jobs, they have made themselves victims. Growing up in Zambia, I saw intelligent people not get into university because they had no money or they did not know anyone in power or authority or because they were not willing to bribe a university official just to get a place. When I moved to the UK it became clear to me that if you put in the work you will get the results you want. A lot of young people in the Welsh valleys and other former mining towns around the UK have been brainwashed by the previous generation; they have been told how the government took away the only work they could do. They were brought up with this victim mentality hence they feel like the whole world is against them and it is stopping them from doing anything better in their lives.

The above example shows that a lot of people are in self-made prisons and they do not really want to get out. They do very little in life but expect life to give them back the best. The amount of success that a person attains in life will always be in proportion to the work that they do. You have to ask yourself: are you working really hard and what do you need to improve? You have to really analyse the quality of your work and look at the results you are producing. If you are not able to get a job for a long time, ask yourself whether you are doing everything that is necessary for you to stand out. After the recession, the competition for the jobs available was very high and you had to really stand out. You have to make sure that you stand out in all you do and in your work. You must remember that every job that you do, no matter how unimportant it might be, might be your opportunity to turn it into bigger and better things in life. Remember everything you do for your employer, you do for yourself. The employer has given you an opportunity to shine and it is up to you to Arise up and shine. You will only be able to do this if you understand that you have to be prepared for every opportunity, even if the opportunity is not there at the moment because you just never know what might happen in the future. Luck is what happens when opportunity meets preparedness, and all the successful people today understand that this is the only way you will ever be successful in life. You have to be prepared all the time in order for you to win; always remember what you get in life is what you put in.

A lot of people are not putting enough into life for them to get back enough to lead a happy life. Imagine a man sat on the heater and telling it to give him heat then he will give it firewood. Everything in life you get is always going to be in proportion with what you put in, nothing more nothing less. So, before you start pointing fingers at people and blaming them for all the misfortunes you have had in life ask yourself this question: have I done enough to be successful? People are too quick to blame other people and they never look at themselves at all. Why have some people come from sleeping in the streets to being multi-millionaires and others have gone from having it all to having nothing at all? We are self-made but only the successful will admit it and if you talk to successful people you will hear the difference in their tones. A successful person will tell you what they did in order to be successful. When they talk to you, you can hear the control they have in all their life situations they found themselves in. They do not blame anyone for any misfortunes they might face. However, unsuccessful people blame it all on other people or circumstances, they take very little or no responsibility at all with what went wrong in their lives. These people might never get back to the top because they will have taken away control of their lives and put it in the hands of other people. They will not be doing what they need to do to change their lives for the better because they won't think that it is their duty to change their lives.

Some people, when they are not blaming circumstances or other people, are busy spending their time not doing anything that will lead them to the life that they want. Imagine a student who is supposed to be studying for his or her exam but is putting off the revision for six months and then has to do a year's work the night before. The fact is, it is too late to do the quality of work needed to be done in order to be successful. In our final year of university, we had to choose from certain topics we wanted to do in the exam. There were eight questions about all of the topics we had done and we had to choose two out of the eight. The day before the exam I was in the library and two people I knew very well—we also went to the same high school—were doing their last-minute revision. Talking to them, I realised they were doing a topic that was not going to be in the exam. They had to quickly choose a new topic and try to learn it all in 12 hours.

Why do we want to do this to ourselves? There seems to be a lot of things to do today and a lot of people have forgotten to look after the most important things in life. They are caught up in living in the moment, so much so that they can't even have time to think about the future. To be prepared for an event you have to make sure you make time to prepare for these opportunities. You have to make sure you find quiet moments to set your goal; if you do not have a goal, you are not really going anywhere. Remember success is a progressive realisation of worthy ideals; you have to be aiming somewhere if you are to be successful. Remember success is not a destination but a journey, a journey that should be taken from your first to final breath on earth. You should ensure that you make time to work on your goals. You need to check your progress and see how near you are to your goal. If you do not make time to check your progress you might as well be blindfolded for the rest of your life. Time is precious but a lot of people don't know that and as a result they do not use it wisely. For you to *Arise and Shine*, you must ensure you spend time developing your knowledge and skill in whatever you want to go into. Les Brown once said if you spend five years studying a particular topic, each day by the end of the five-year period you will become one of the leading experts in that field.

You, however, have to understand that bad times will come in your quest to fulfil your dream and how you respond to this will determine where you end up in life. People go through similar setbacks but how you respond to these will determine where you end up in life. I was in a class of people who did not do well in their high school exams but we have ended up in different places in life. How did that happen? It's because of the choices we made; I had made up my mind I was going to university even though a lot of people never thought that it was possible for me. Failing is part of life, but if you fail it does not mean that you should give up because there is always tomorrow to start all over again. When I was in primary school I would throw away all the pages where I did not get 100%, and sometimes we have to forget these days. People may remind you that you failed, but you have a choice to focus on that what is to come in the future as long as you keep striving onwards and press forwards until you reach you goal. It's always too soon to give up on your dreams, no matter what has gone on in the past – you can still make it but only if you believe that you have the power to change the future. The past is gone and you cannot do anything to change it, even if you try, so what is the point in looking back when you can't do anything about it?

I was listening to a conversation and this woman I knew well was talking about how her mother was the worst mother in the world and she went around telling many people how bad her mother was and how she made her life hell. Now this woman is nearly sixty years old and she is still talking about what happened nearly four decades ago. This woman has children whom she loves dearly and grandchildren who really adore her. If you were looking from the outside, you would see the future is bright, but she does not see things that way. She looks at all the things that happened to her many years ago. A lot of people hold on to the past so they can use it as an excuse when things go wrong. Why do you want to let something that happened many years ago destroy your life? You should just look at what you have today and decide you can start.

Remember you have to start to be great and if you are constantly revisiting the past you will never move on.The founding father of psychology in America William James once said; "We become what we think about" if you are not thinking about what your future has for you there is no way you are going to be successful in your life because the past will be holding you back. The past tells you that you cannot do this and that, but if you are looking ahead you will aim to find solutions to all the things that hold you back. Let go of the past and you will reach your goal in life. If you are holding on to your past you will just become an average person and if you are an average person you can easily slip below that average. You have to aim to create new stories in your life and don't waste your time looking back at all the things that went well or did not go so well in the past. You can only let go of the past by spending time developing yourself. A lot of people will spend time doing anything in the world apart from spending time on making themselves better. It is important that we make time to develop ourselves. A lot of people want to live a better life but they do not want to make time to develop their skills; you have to make your own time for this.

You may be a very talented individual but if you do not develop your talent, someone less talented than you will achieve more in life. You have to be prepared to spend as much time as it takes to make yourself better in the job. A lot of people are not successful in life because they have stopped educating themselves; the truth is that education in life does not and should not stop once you leave school or university. Education should carry on through life because there will always be something to learn and the people that understand this principle are the people who are known as successful.

You should aim to do better than your best all the time. You should never settle in your life because the world is constantly changing. Your best today might be what you need to do, but if you do the exact thing in a year's time it might not be good enough anymore. You have to keep developing yourself and if you want to be successful, you have to make time to analyse and develop your skills. You have to really think of what you are doing, this is the only way you are going to learn what you need to improve on. A lot of people do not realise they are not doing what they were born to do because they do not spend time evaluating where they are in life and check what their strongest skills are. If you do not find out what your strongest skills are, you will not reach that Promised Land. You want to do the things that give you pleasure and pure joy in your life. If you do the things you really love, you will get up every morning with purpose and determination to do what you were created to do. Remember, you did not just show up here to amount to nothing; you were born to win and no one else will find that winning formula for your life except you. And remember, you can if you think you can!

A lot of people do not realise that life is a river full of unlimited opportunities; some people go to this river with a bucket and draw out as much as they can, others with a cup and others just a spoon – believe it or not. Opportunities are all around us and they are sometimes wrapped up as problems of daily life. You should never dwell too much on what you are going through because you have the power to change it all. However, a lot of people do not realise that whatever they are going through at this moment in time they have the power to change it. Some dwell too much on all the things that are going wrong to the extent that they end up missing out on opportunities out there. The moment you decide that you are going to go for what you want in life is the moment you begin being successful.

Who do i Consider to be a successful person? A successful person is a mother who does not work but does a very good job at being a mother and wife and she does it because that's what she wants to do. A successful person is a teacher who goes to work because he wants to change and impact on other people's lives. A successful person is someone who goes to a job they enjoy and loves very much and they wake up every morning full of joy and anticipation. You have a choice to stay where you are or move on but a lot of people do not really believe they have a choice and so spend a decade doing a job they do not love at all. We were all created to do something; we did not just show up here so that we can amount to nothing. We were born to win but some people have made a choice to be losers. Now that is a little harsh don't you think? No! I do not.

Reason number one is that a lot of people are trying to be successful by doing all the things that made them fail in the past; if you know that something does not work why on earth try and do it? For you to be successful you have to look at your own strategy. For example, I had to look at my own study strategy for me to produce the results that I wanted.

The second point is that certain people want everything to be just the way they want it to be and if it is different they will not do it. You have to be flexible because sometimes you will have to go along paths which were not part of your plan, but if you keep that goal in mind, you will get there. The best thing of going along all the unexpected paths is that you pick certain things which will make you stronger; failing my high school exams taught me that it's not really over until I win. Going to university was a life opportunity and even though I was struggling academically, I still saw the opportunities that were there for me if endured to the end.

Remember: you are going to do the best in your life and something might come up that might turn your life upside down in a twinkling of an eye, even then it is your choice. My fiancée, Suzie, invited me to her church for a charity concert for the Clarence Edu Foundation. Afterwards, I left feeling really motivated. Clarence was involved in a car accident in his younger days and he was left paralysed from the neck down. The insurance company found a loophole in the system and they would not pay up and the poor man was left to deal with all the changes in his life without any financial support. He, however, refused to dwell on what happened to him and today he runs his foundation and goes around encouraging other people.

When I see him I always think that he has every right to complain and I think a lot of people would look at him and agree. However, Clarence decided he wanted to be happy. You have to decide you are going to be happy, even when certain things that are really unfair happen. You have to say to yourself: I deserve to be happy and I am going to be happy. You see a lot of people do not look at what they have, they just look at what they do not have. I think Clarence always looked at what he still had left and not what he had lost. He was able to Arise up and shine brightly.

You see, he saw an opportunity to carry on doing what he wanted to do in life and more. I swear that when you hear this man speak you would ask why a lot of people who have a lot going for them do not really make it in life. The answer is this: some people are willing to do today what other people won't in order for them to have what other people won't have tomorrow. Some people go to the river of life with a spoon, others go to a river of life with a cup and other go with a bucket. However, some people go to the river of life with a lot of buckets and they draw out as much as they can, these are the people who are truly successful. The opportunities are all around you and each day you wake up is an opportunity for you to work on the possibilities that will surround you throughout the day.

One the most important things is that the people you see every day in your life are going to help you realise your possibilities. Zig Ziglar once said: "Just help as many people as possible to get what they want and you will also get what you want." The question is how does that work? This is how this principle works. Firstly, imagine you are running a business. Your customer wants the best customer service possible and if you give this, they will keep coming to your business and encourage other people to come to your business. Now put this in terms of personal relationships: what do people want in other people? They want to work with people they can trust, they want to work with people who are helpful. What happens is that when you help others get what they want, they will help you get what you want in your life or your job.

When there is a promotion in the workplace, the first thing that most managers look at is who works well with other people or who is able to get other employees to do extra work when required. A lot of people are not successful because on their journey to be successful they are only focusing on what they want and do not really look at what other people around them want. You have to care for other people's needs on your journey to be successful; a lot of people do not realise that they will need people to support them on the way to their destination. You will never be successful, no matter what your abilities are, if you have a bad attitude towards people. These people will not support you when you need their support. I think this is the downfall of a lot of people: they think that they have to think about themselves all the time, but they do not realise that they will need other people to reach their dreams.

Here is a common example. You are looking for a job doing something you love, but you just cannot find one in that field. Then a person you know very well tells you they have a relative who is looking for someone with your qualifications and abilities. Do you think if you did not get on with people they would have recommended you for the job? Well we know the answer: it is a big fat no. Just help as many others get what they want and you will get what you want also.

You can change your life only if you want to. There are a lot of people who are waiting for tomorrow to come. I remember when I was growing up in Zambia I knew a shop owner who put a sign up saying 'if you want credit, come tomorrow.' The thing was that this sign was always there the next day. A lot of people are treating their lives in the same way. They always say they will start tomorrow, but the truth my friends is that tomorrow never comes. If you have a dream, start working on it now, stop waiting for the perfect time.

Stop waiting for the perfect moment or for tomorrow, do it now. The truth is that a lot of people are looking for the world to change then they will change. They do not realise that they are the change they are looking for. While some people are waiting for the world to change, other people are changing the world. The time to do what you want to do in your life is now; if you wait for the perfect time you will never do anything great in life because there isn't such a thing as a perfect moment. You have to do what you want to do now. One of my friends was always talking about all the things he wanted to do and he has been waiting for the perfect time to do it ever since we left school and he has still not done anything, a true example of tomorrow never comes.

To conclude this chapter, we are self-made but only the successful admit it. We have all the power we need to reach our goals in life, but the majority of people only use up a very low percentage of their power. You have to understand that there is only one person who can change your life for the better: do not look at someone else in the world to change because the only person who can change it is you. I believe that everyone was born to win but other people do not realise that if they work hard in life and do what is necessary for them to win, there is nothing that is going to stop them. You have to understand that most of the things that happen in our lives could have been changed if you had taken actions in the first place. I ended up being a graduate not by accident but because I wanted to change the course of my life. I realised that there was only one person who could change my life for the better and that was me so I took constructive actions to change my life. You have to take action to change your life; do not spend your life doing what you were not born to do. You shall know the truth and the truth shall set you free. The truth is that life is a river of opportunities; you can draw out of it as much as you wish and people will not stop you. Unlike natural rivers, rivers of life will never go dry and this river is around us in whatever you are doing. Stop looking for problems in your life and start looking for solutions. If you take control of your life and run it just the way you want to, you will definitely reach your goals. You should have a clear plan of what you want in your life and believe that only you can do it. You have to really believe that you deserve the best in life and only you can change your life. The river of life has a lot of opportunities for us. So, drop what you are doing and run to it because no one will carry you there. Only you can, and when you get there, draw out as much as you can. Only you can decide how much you will draw out. If you draw as much as is possible then you will *Arise and Shine*!

Chapter 4

An Unknown Heaven

As a Christian, I find myself imagining what heaven will be like and I think of how beautiful a place it will be. I imagine all the good things that will be there and this fills me with so much joy and longing. The truth is I know very little about this place, but the whole idea of a place that is filled with happiness fills me with joy I cannot express. We are all on a journey to find success and to do what we were born to do. Trials and tribulations will come our way but if we continue striving, we will reach the Promised Land we are looking for. A lot of people have been looking for success all their lives but what they don't realise is that they are surrounded by the success they are looking for each and every day. A lot of time we are where we are in our life because we want to stick to what we know and are comfortable with. But if the life we know is one that we are not comfortable with and is not bringing us success, then we will not be successful. You cannot do the self-same thing and expect different results; you will continue getting the same results and you will end up exactly where you are. If you want to see results, you have to step out of your comfort zone and do something you are not comfortable with: that is the only way you are going to grow. I once heard Les Brown say "an unknown heaven is better than a known hell" and the current crisis in the Italian ports where migrants are arriving in their thousands risking their lives after a very dangerous journey comes to mind. Why would people want to risk their lives just go to Europe? I answered this myself: An unknown Heaven is always going to be better than a known a hell.

So, if we know that there is always going to be something better in our life, if we are willing to go beyond what we are currently doing, then that is the direction we need to go in. A lot of people are doing just enough to not get fired and they are just about keeping their jobs and a roof over their heads. What if they worked a little bit harder in their jobs and became more valuable to the business? I think a lot of people do not do this because they conform to their peers. A lot of people do not want to be seen to be doing something different to what other people are doing. I saw this a lot in school, a lot of people were just doing what everyone else was doing, people used to laugh at the same unfunny jokes, but because everyone was laughing a lot of people just joined in.

The idea of standing alone scares a lot of people because they feel if they are different then there is something wrong with them. I found that being different meant I was left out of a lot of things in school because I was regarded as strange by other people. When you are working on your dream a lot of people will think you are strange, a lot of people will tell you that it is not possible and will laugh at you for having a dream or for even daring to dream. This was the hell I knew and I did not like it at all. I wanted to do something that would fill me with so much joy, but what I was doing at that moment was not.

When that fateful day in August 2007 arrived, a dream was born because I wanted to live in this heaven that was unknown to me. It was a heaven I thought was going to fill me with so much happiness. I did not know how it felt to do well in an exam or to have a goal to strive towards, but I was going to do this because it sounded a little bit better than the place I knew, which I hated. I thought I could do better if only I did something different to what I had been doing. From that day on I was willing to do what I had never done before and that was to stand alone and do what I wanted to do. A lot of people are not really doing what they were born to do; they do a lot of things in life apart from that one thing they desire deeply to do. I believe that if a lot of people were to step out of their comfort zone, they would be doing what they were born to do and the world will be a better a place for it. However, what we have is a lot of people who take all their talents with them to the grave. Someone I know well told me that the richest place you will find on earth is the graveyard because there you will find all the unfinished novels and pieces of music. You are going to find talents that were not used at all.

The question is: why do a lot of people take all their greatness to the grave with them? I think the reason that a lot of people do not manifest their greatness is because of fear. Zig Ziglar describes fear as "false evidence appearing real". A lot of people are so scared to do something they are not comfortable with. I read a quote by Sir Winston Churchill that says: "the only thing that you must fear is fear itself." I saw this quote when I was with one of my close friends and he made a remark, something along the lines of that does not really make much sense at all. It made a lot of sense to me because, ladies and gentlemen, fear stops you from doing all the things you really want. Fear stops you from leaving an abusive relationship because you are worried about being alone forever; fear stops you doing the thing you really want to do. The only way you can ever be successful is if you take action; a lot of people are not where they want to be in life because they are paralysed by fear. They are not happy where they are but the idea of doing something they have never done scares them. There is only one way to overcome fear and that is doing the thing that you are scared of. Unless you take action, you will always be scared to do anything in life. The truth is that a lot of people are not where they want to be because they are scared to make that first step. Have you ever thought what is really going to happen if you do what you are most fearful of? You get to live your dream; you get to live a very fulfilling life. Can you imagine waking up every day doing something that you really love doing, working every day with a purpose. A lot of people would love to do something but they have not got the courage to overcome the fears that they have. The question is: why do a lot of people just settle so low in life and do not do anything to better their lives? Why are they paralysed by fear so much that they are not really living at all?

I think the answer to this question is that a lot of people are worried about losing whatever little they have. Being one of the youngest people in work has its advantages because I get to learn why people do certain things. I have noticed that a lot of people are worried about losing everything that they have if they pursue their dreams. I hear people saying that they would have loved to do this but were worried what would happen if it never really worked out. This is the question that everyone asks: what happens if it does not work out? However, there is another question that only the successful people ask: what if it does work out? What if leaving your current job is the best thing that will ever happen to your life? You do not have to think about failing, you just have to use the abilities that you have been given to make it work. You have to really believe that you were born to be happy.

A lot of people do not really believe that good things are supposed to happen to them. Good things are really supposed to happen to you and they will if you get out of your comfort zone. Sometimes you have to risk it all. A friend's sister fell in love with a man who was not of the same culture or religion, but because she loved him and he made her happy she went ahead and married him. The marriage caused a lot of trouble in the family and some of the family members do not speak to her family because of it. She knew how much joy and happiness they would share together, so much so that she was willing to risk it all. A lot of people are not willing to risk it all, they have so little in their hands but all they need to do is throw that away and hold on to something great. Let go of the little thing in your hand and grab onto something great, something that will bring you pure joy and happiness. My friend's sister's parents supported her in the end but she was willing to risk it all. Are you willing to risk that job you do not like for something you love? Are you risking leaving an abusive relationship for a single and happy life? Are you willing to give up everything that you have to go find true happiness? The truth is a lot of people won't; they will stay in the known hell all the days of their lives and we will all suffer because we will not be able to see their great talents and abilities because they are scared of exchanging the little they have for a lot more.

For a long time, I was scared of being successful and what it could do to my life. I always looked at the responsibilities that being successful might bring. I looked at a lot of people who seemed to be on their feet at all times and I would say I would not be able to do that, or I would not want to be as successful as that. I look back now and I think I made those sorts of judgements because I did not know what those people had to go through in life to get where they are in their professional career and their personal life. I did not know how much free time they had in their lives. Success is available to all human beings and it's up to each and every one of us to decide how much we will draw out from this river of life.

Some people have gone to the river of life with a little tea spoon and they got out very little, only because they are afraid of drawing a lot in case they get very successful. A lot of people wonder if they will be able to handle the amount of responsibility that being very successful will bring. What these people do not realise is that success is a journey and not a destination. This means that on this journey you are going to learn everything that you need to know in order for you to do what you are doing successfully. The question that you must ask yourself is: do you want to have a lot of responsibility or do you want to have what other will not have? I think I would rather have a lot of responsibility and be able to afford my mortgage rather than having very little responsibility. The fear of success has resulted in lot of people setting their bars too low in life and they have hit them and they do not realise what they are missing out on. I have heard a lot of people say money is not everything and I think, to some extent, money is not everything but it plays an important part in living a successful life. People have killed for money, marriages have ended because of lack of money. If you work hard and honestly, you deserve to have a lot of money and be very successful. Do not be afraid of success: you deserve it.

The sad fact is that people who are afraid of success make a decision not to grow and if you are not growing, you achieve very little. People who have made a decision not to grow do just enough not to get fired. They end up doing the job that they hate with a passion all their life. After I left university someone said; "Welcome to the adult world and, by the way, you will have to work most of it." In Chapters One and Two we spoke about our friend who would have been a designer but ended up doing the job she never liked for 25 years; wasted years and talent. A lot of people are not doing what they were born to do; they are waiting for other people to tell them what they are good at and what they are not good at. I believe too many people are not able to grow because they are not doing what they were born to do and the results show.

You have to stand for what you believe you were born to do. A lot of people were told a lot of times they were not good enough but they just strove on and overcame it all. You have to ask yourself how much am I growing as a person or how much am I growing in my current job. If you discover that you are not growing, you have to ask yourself a few more questions. The first question is: are you really doing the best or are you leaving a lot more in the tank? Are you learning enough about your field? The truth of the matter is a lot of people, once they are employed, stop learning all together. What they do not realise is that learning does not stop at all. A lot of people are stuck in life because their knowledge has reached its limit. A lot of people have made a decision not to grow because of fear of getting successful and having a lot of responsibilities and this has in turn limited their own abilities.

Remember the more successful you become, the more aware you will become about the job you are doing. When you become great in your job, you would have had to grow into it and would have learnt a lot for you to become great anywhere. Make sure that every day you strive to take a step that will make you grow. I knew an older man who could not speak a word of English and all he did was learn three words a day of English and in five years his English was immaculate. If you are afraid of doing a certain job, go ahead and do it. Do not be afraid of success because you will grow into it; the boots of success are not too big for anyone who has been preparing for it. All you have to do is become more prepared in the job that you are doing. You have to have a plan of what you want to become in your life. The truth of the matter is that a lot of people have made up their minds not be great. If we decide not to grow we are giving up on life all together. We do not want to be like those people who reach the end of their lives only to realise that they have never lived at all. You are alive so that you can grow, arise and start the journey today because everything that you need to know is on this road to success.

Others do not grow because they are scared of failure hence they don't try to attempt anything that makes them remotely uncomfortable. I remember when I failed my high school exams, one of the fears I carried with me was failing again. Even though I was doing a lot of things very well, I was very scared of failing and this was affecting me in a lot of things I was doing. The great Zig Ziglar once said that failure is just a detour and not a dead-end road. A lot of people have made failure out to be a dead-end road and they have not done anything worthwhile in their lives. The fear of failure has made a lot of people not want to attempt to do anything great in their lives.

I think the biggest irony is that people who do not try anything in their lives because they do not want to be seen as failures just end up being exactly that. I believe that a lot of people have talked themselves out of doing great things in their lives because their fear of failure is greater than their desire. Failing my exam changed my life for the better as I became a new person all together. Author and motivational speaker Tony Robbins said: "Success is not what you have, it's what you become because of it."

We might fail time after time but if we keep going, we become problem solvers and we are able to handle all the difficult situations that we might face in the future. If you have the attitude of believing that no matter how hard, no matter how bad it gets I am going to make it – you will make it. I believe that people who do not make it in life are not willing to fail their way to success. They think that people who made it to the top are too perfect, but what they forget is that you do not have to be great to get started, you have to get started to be great. Les Brown once said something I thought was very interesting: "Anything that is worth doing, is worth doing badly." I can hear someone saying; "But Frank if you do it badly, you will not get any satisfaction from it." If you do not know how to do something then you will not be able to do it perfectly until you learn. You will feel the fear when you start a new thing but the important thing you should always remember is doing it anyway. You might have a goal you want to achieve in life and if you endeavoured to reach it, even if it's not your calling, you would have enough preparation to do what you were born to do with so much confidence. Any time the fear of failing comes into your mind you should always tell yourself this: "I will fail my way to success, I do not have to be great to get started, I have to get stared to be great."

The other thing that makes a lot of people stay where they are in life is that they do not want to walk on a road that will make them feel lonely. A lot of people will follow the crowd because they think that if everyone is doing it, then it must be right. If you are walking on a road that feels like it is a lonely one and you wonder why you are the only one on it, the answer is because you are dancing to the sound of your own drum, your Destiney. You have to do what you are born to do and not what everyone else is doing. This is very difficult for a lot of people because they want to feel they have support all the time. A lot of people think that if they do something different to what other people are doing, they will not have the support of their friends and family. However, what they do not realise is that if they run for their dream, they will have other people supporting them on their journey; they will be supported by other successful people. Why would you want someone else to support your failures in life? The people you allow to be supportive in your life should be people who are building you up along the way and making you a better person. You might be standing alone but if you are building yourself to become a better person, you will only become successful if you create a better you. Do not be afraid to walk alone because the reward that is awaiting you is great. Zig Ziglar in one of his speeches once said: "There are no traffic jams on the extra mile because very few people are willing to go that extra mile hence very few people can really count themselves as having been very successful." Do not be afraid because your road feels lonely because that road was created for only you.

A lot of people do not achieve all their dreams because they want to do things they feel comfortable with and things they know very well. There is saying that goes: "It's better the devil you know." I have always wondered about this saying. I ask myself why people really believe that this is the best they can do in life? We were all born to win and we do not have to stay on the side lines and watch other people succeed while staying on the bottom of the pyramid. I believe that a lot of people have not achieved much in life because they do not venture to unknown lands because they are comfortable with what they have and they do not really want to risk it all.

A lot of people will watch other people get what they want in life and wish they could have what the successful people have, they spend all day wishing they could be as successful as this one and the other. A lot of people spend a lot of time wishing they could be successful but the truth of the matter is that they can be. They can be what they want to be if only they do something they have never done before. If you are doing something that has made you fail in life over and over again, it's time to change your tactics and do something you have never done before. If you have not been a hard worker, it's time you put in some hours for free and show your employers what you are capable of. You have to do something that you are really scared of as Susan Jeffers in her book says: "feel the fear and do it anyway". That's all you have to do, just carry on doing what you need to do.

When things start to get uncomfortable you have to still keep going. I travelled on a very bad road on my way to boarding school when I was in Zambia. The roads were very bad and all I wanted to do was to get out of the car, but I could not do that, I had to wait till we reached the destination. I remember the first week of boarding school was very exciting, so much so it did not matter how you got there you were just happy to get there and it did not matter how bad the journey was you were just happy to share in the joy with all your mates. Life's journey can be like that; the road will be bumpy and the journey may be long, but when you get there you will find rest, happiness and pure joy.

A lot of people have, however, let the hardships that they face destroy what was made only for them. They do not realise their greatness and they take it to the grave with them. The journey might be long and hard, but the only way you are going to make your life easier is if you do the things you are afraid of doing. If you think the journey to success is hard, imagine the journey of living in mediocrity; you will not be doing anything you want to do, which will render you unhappy; you will not be giving the best in your job, which will not make you a very dependable person. Imagine this: you have been working for a company for a very long time and you have that one thing inside you that has remained unused for years because you feel you do not want to embarrass yourself. In the fear, you do not realise the company needs that thing you are holding inside you; you have a key to a lot of the answers that management is looking for. However, you are holding back because you do not believe you are good enough or you do not want to take a risk.

What you have stored in your subconscious mind will appear real even though it is not real. You have probably been feeding your mind negative things all your life and what you need to do is feed your conscious mind positive things and your positive mind will think you are good enough. I imagine you are in that place today, standing in front of the managers and telling them your good idea and you are becoming a very valuable member of the organisation. A lot of people are not what they are born to be because they have a massive inferiority complex; they believe that they are not good enough for anything and they always settle for the lowest things in life. However, they do not realise that only they can do the things that they fear and they can become changed people. In other words, to be what you want to be, you have to do something you have never done before.

A lot of people are scared of doing anything in their lives because they are scared of what their friends are going to say if they do a particular thing. So, in order to impress their friends, they do what their friends are telling them to do. A lot of people are afraid of doing the opposite to what those close to them say because they do not want to go through the humiliation of having been told not do that thing but going ahead anyway and it not being a success. Tony Robins once said "that success is not what you have at the end of a particular project or goal", it is who you become. You might fail in your goal but you will have discovered what your real calling in life is, it will have made you a stronger person and prepared you for the future. You have to look at the people you are getting your advice from; a lot of people spend a lot of their time listening to people who have never tried anything in life. If you think about it, how can someone who has never tried to better their life by going to places they fear tell you what to do? A lot of people listen to these people and, in the end, they end up not going anywhere in life. I believe that if a lot of people listened to themselves more than they listen to what other people are saying, a lot more people would be successful. However, this is not the case. A lot of people are always listening to what other people are saying, trying to impress people they do not even like every day – what a complete waste of time.

You were born to win and whatever you have in you, no matter how far-fetched it might seem to be at the time, there is a reason that you have that dream inside you. You have to go for it no matter how many people say it has never been done. I don't think that the fact that something has not been done is a good excuse for not doing it; you can be the first person to do it. After all, everything that has ever been created by man was first of all stated by one person and remember what Les Brown said: "you have greatness within you!"

I have noticed that a lot of people do not enjoy life because they are looking at what they have now. As I mentioned at the start of the chapter, I am a Christian and this idea of an unknown heaven really fascinates me. Growing up in Africa, I saw a lot of people who had very little, but the idea that one day they will have all their heart desires helped them enjoy a really good life even though they had very little going for them. You have to have a goal in life for you to have a successful life and you must only focus on that goal. A lot of people focus on what is going on now and they make all their decisions based on what is going on at the moment and forget that there is tomorrow. If you have a goal in life, you will always focus on that goal even when things get really difficult and I think that the reason that a lot of people fail in life is because they have not set goals; a lack of goals means that they do not really know where they are going. You have to get up today and start walking towards that goal. Many people have parked up on their dream because the journey just seems too long and hard. My advice to anyone working on a particular goal in life is keep going, you do not have to park up and settle. Earl Nightingale reminds us that success is progressive realisation of a worthy goal, so if you do something you are afraid to do, you are already successful. Therefore, if you have a goal, work at it with all your heart like your life depends on it because it does, and if you do what you are afraid of doing, life is really going to be better on the other side.

So, if your life depends on it, why do a lot of people refuse to leave situations that do not make them happy?

The truth is a lot of people cannot see themselves beyond where they are at the moment. They have every excuse in the world why they cannot leave a bad a job or a bad marriage. That's all they are, excuses, not reasons for not doing what they really what to do. One day on the train coming from work, I was sat next to two men and one was talking about why he couldn't afford to divorce his wife. He spoke about all the benefits of him not leaving the marriage even though he was not happy. A lot of people live a life of looking at the benefits that they get from very unhappy situations. The truth is that a lot of people do not realise that the prize you get for leaving things that are not making you happy behind you is peace of mind and freedom to enjoy your life. Les Brown once told a story of a soldier captured in battle and he was due to face the firing squad. The captain, however, gave him two choices; he could either face the firing squad or go through the door of unknown horrors. He chose to face the firing squad. After the shots had rung out, the captain's secretary asked him what was beyond this door. He said: "Freedom. But a lot of people do not take it because they do not know what is there." They do not realise that if they leave the job they hate so much and find something they love, they will enjoy their lives a lot more than they are today. A lot of people are not doing what they really want to be doing in life because they just do not see themselves beyond what they are doing today.

The truth is, when pursuing your dreams, it is going to be hard, it is not easy and a lot of people have given up. Sometimes you will do everything you have to do to be successful and something unexpected will happen to you, but that is life and everyone goes through setbacks of one or other. Remember that whatever you are going through at the moment has not come to stay, it has come to pass, what you need to do is keep going. I am reminded of a famous song *You'll Never Walk Alone*. The chorus of this song says, "Walk on through the rain, walk on through the storm, though your dreams be tossed and blown, walk on, walk on!" Just walk on.

The idea that you will have to do a lot of things in order for you to be successful really puts off many people. All you have to do is keep holding your head up high. Remember that you have to fail your way to success. You might not know how you are going to do it, but if you carry on learning and moving towards that goal, it will be revealed to you as you carry on your journey. You will find people who will say that you are not good enough; door after door will shut in your face but as long as you keep your head up high, you will make it. You have to look at your plan over and over again; imagine what your life will be like if you reach that goal. You have to focus on that goal and that goal alone. If that goal is there every day through the storm, through the rain, you will keep going. Remember the rain and storm have not come to stay, they have come to pass.

However, I think that a lot of people do not make it through the rain and the storm because they look at their lives and they just think they are not good enough. Have you ever sat in room with a grade one violinist? They produce the worst sound in the world, all you want to do is get out of the room. However, come and listen to the student in three weeks' time; the sound will be very different. If you were to listen to the same student six to twelve months along the way, the sound would be even better. Life can be like that as well. When we start a new thing, we will not be very good at it, but if we carry on doing it, we will get better at it. A lot of people, however, do not get started at all because they do not think they are good enough. There are countless talented authors who think they cannot be good enough. I worked with a guy who was a good writer but he thought he could not have competed with great authors like Robert Ludlum. So, what did he do? He packed away all his hard work. And there, ladies and gentlemen, is another great talent lost to the world. We are so afraid that we are not going to be as great as the people we look up to, when the truth of the matter is that they were not born as great as they are known today; one day they were like a grade one violinist. So, all you have to do is get started and keep on working on the goal, believe it is possible. Nothing is impossible. One of my close friends always says that impossible is just two letters too long and also that the word impossible itself says 'I'm possible.' You do not have to be great to get started, you have to get started to be great.

For a long time in my high school life, I always argued for my limitations. I really believed I was not very good at anything and I would have told you why I thought I was not good at anything. I had low self-esteem from as far back as I can remember. I thought I was really different from all the kids in school. I never believed I was special, I never believed that I had a great talent within me. I was looking at all the things that I was not good at. Too many people are always looking at all the things that they are not good at all the time therefore they forget the things they are good at. Sometimes we are not good at certain aspects of life simply because we were not born to do that particular thing. Your own heaven is waiting for you, but you are just looking at what other people are good at hence you remain in a known hell. You should stop comparing yourself with other people if you are going to be successful. You need to focus on the things you are really good at and stop looking at all the things you are not good at.

Every institution you can think of has different people with different skill sets; having people who are good but have different skills is the thing that has made every successful organisation as successful as they are. I always say it's good to have more than one skill in life, you have to have a few skills to compete in today's job market. However, you should make sure that you do not become a jack of all trades and a master of none. Be what you want to be and do not focus on all the things that you are not good at and nurture the talent that you have. You can win if you do what you are really good at. One of our priests is very good at a lot of things; I have noticed he can have a conversation about almost everything with just about anyone. Some people are just good like that. I am his deacon and I am not good at talking and I will probably never be that good. But I tell you what, I am glad I have someone like that priest to teach me. I get a lot of tips from him and this helps me to develop the skills that I am good at. You have to develop the skills you have got. Do not look at what other people have. A lot of people are scared of applying for higher positions in their work place, they want to be with people who know very little. The idea that they will be in a room full of people with great knowledge puts them off from applying for these jobs. What they do not realise is that working with people with great knowledge will help them in the long run. Remember, if there is no enemy within, the enemy outside will cause us no harm at all.

When you limit your greatness, when the trouble of life comes, you will fall easily. When I was in my second year of university I suffered from depression. This was a very crazy time of my life and busy as well. I remember waking up one day and I just did not want to get up and a few days later I knew I was depressed. My fiancée, Suzie, was living in Gloucester at the time, where we both now live. I remember going to see her and all I could do was sleep. I had a dream of going to university and graduating, now here I was, depressed with assignments to write and exams to revise for. I think this was a defining point of my life; everything I had worked for was going to amount to something or nothing, depending on how I was going to respond. I went to see my doctor and he gave me tablets that made me even more depressed. Exam time was looming and I had to get going. I thought of the unknown heaven which I could only dream of and I decided then that I had to get back on my bike and continue riding; the prize that was awaiting me was greater than staying in the situation I was in at the time.

I threw away the tablets that very moment, went back to the library and was back on the road to my dream. I refused to remain in the known hell and miss out on glorious unknown events that were to come in the future. Whatever you do, make sure that you do not get stuck on what is going on at the present time. Focus on what is awaiting you. Remember whatever you are going through now has not come to stay, it has come to pass; you are only going through a moment. You will come out at the end with so much strength enabling you to overcome whatever future obstacles come.

A lot of people do not make it in life because they do not have faith that things will work out. I heard someone say that seeing is believing, and a lot of people really believe this. What happens when people believe this is that they do not believe things will work out if they cannot see the results or how the problem is going to be solved. A lot of people do not achieve their dreams because they do not see what they have. The only time someone says to someone I wish I could have been like you is when they believe they are good enough. You just have to have faith and keep moving. When I used to sing with the Risca Male Choir in Wales, one of the men, who saw that I was struggling, said to me in the words of Martin Luther King Jr: "In life you have to keep running. If you cannot run just walk, if you cannot walk just crawl, but whatever happens never stop moving".

One of my favourite passages in the Bible says: "You shall see by faith and not by sight." You see, a lot of people do not realise that you have to learn and learn and learn, only then will you able to see properly. Life can be like going up a hill and you will only see the view once you get up at the top. You do not stop because you cannot see what is at the top or even wonder if it will all be worth it. Believing is seeing and you might not physically see what you are achieving at the moment. Remember this, if you carry on, you will see what awaits you; if you see to believe, you only see what is going on in the present time and not the possibilities that your future will bring. You will continue living in a known hell because you are just scared or not able to see the known heaven by faith.

While we are on this theme of an unknown heaven, I would like to tell you about how a simple hobby changed my life. I had been thinking of joining Risca Male Choir for quite some time but I did not have the courage to go through with it. I never felt welcome in most places I had been and I hated that feeling. I had spent just over two years with Risca RFC and I never really felt like I was part of the gang. I really love singing and the sound the choir produced was glorious. I went to a lot of concerts the choir performed and I would just marvel at the sound and wished I could be a part of it. However, I just did not want to be rejected again so I did not go. One Saturday evening I had the courage to phone the Musical Director at the time whose name was Martin Hodson; he was to play a very key role in my self-development in the following few years. He sounded okay on the phone so I decided I would go to one of their practices. I had told myself that I would go for one practice and then no one would ever see me again. I had to get a bus so I got there before anyone else and I wondered what the welcome was going to be like. I sat there asking myself how the members were going to receive this young black man in front of them. I had played all the outcomes in my head and none of them were good. I waited for the members to come in, it felt like a long time. Maybe it was because I was 90 minutes early. The first few members started coming in and one of the senior members invited me in and had a chat with me.

It was my first encounter with a baritone by the name of Gordon; he gave me the best welcome anyone had ever given me before. It was incredible because, five minutes earlier, I was wondering why I had even bothered. After a few seconds of chatting to this man, I knew that I wanted to be part of the choir. Martin walked in the room, he was as nice and polite as he was on the phone and it was a done deal for me: I was going to be part of the choir. I watched the first half of the practice; I was up close in person with the men I had heard for three years previously. I held my tears back as I realised that I had a chance to be part of something special. I asked myself why I had not come earlier but it did not matter, I was here now. I had my voice test with Martin when the choir took a break, I told him I was a second tenor but after doing my voice test he said I was a top tenor. Now I would like to remind you that at this point I had not been top in anything in my life before and, even though I knew top tenor was a section and not a special position in the choir, it was special for me to be top anything. When Martin said that I was not a second tenor but a top tenor, I translated that as: you are better than you think you are. The journey to where I am today really began on my first day at the choir headquarters. I was to enjoy four wonderful years with the choir and met a lot of great people and because the majority of the people were older than me, I got to learn a lot from them.

Four days after joining the choir I got my exam results for my first year of sixth form, which I passed with flying colours and I spent the evening of my results singing with Risca Male Choir. The dream of going to university was truly on. After about a month or two with the choir, I went to Martin's house and he was surprised because I did not know the song "Can You Feel the Love Tonight" and I was too embarrassed to say that, even though I was 18 years old, I had not seen *The Lion King* yet but we sang through it anyway. I started going for lessons once a week at Martin's house and every day my voice got better and better. I would go home and practise all the new techniques to my brother's anguish. The highlight for me came when I sang two solos in 2010 at a small concert raising money for a concert we were going to have later that year. Standing in front of that church and hearing people cheering me after I had sung was great.. People told me how nice my voice was and this really improved my confidence. I went to school the following Monday and one of my teachers told me something had changed. I truly believe that on that day the old me started making way for a new me. I was able to say I was good at something; I was not the best singer in the room by any stretch of the imagination but I was happy with own performance. Because I was happy with my own performance that afternoon I started learning to be happy with my own performance in a lot of other things.

One thing that I learnt when I was in the choir was that easy was not an option. We, as a choir, sang some really challenging pieces. I remember Gordon saying to me that I had to practice not just once a week but every day. What a lot of people did not know is that I have an eye condition called Nystagmus, which is an involuntary movement of the eye. I struggled to read the music so I would go home and practise note by note, word by word, and put them all my in my head. This experience taught me that if there is problem, there will always be a solution. I used that in my schoolwork and it paid off. I use this technique even today to solve my work and personal problems. The trouble with a lot of people is that they will always look at the problem and not the solution. I knew what the problem was and I found a way to solve the problem through being part of the choir that I was scared of joining in the first place. The benefits of being in the choir were huge for me; I made a lot of friendships and I met people who helped me on life's journey until I graduated from university. None of them knew it but they were helping me along to greatness.

One September evening whilst waiting to get on stage, I overhead one of my fellow top tenors, Paul, talking about work. I was looking for a place to go for work experience so I asked him what he did and he said he was a Human Resources manager. My eyes lit up because I was doing a degree in Business and Human Resources and I was looking for a place to do work experience and I could not find one anywhere. I had to ask him, and he did what he could and he got me the work experience that I badly needed. A lot of my fellow students at university could not find anything at all, but I did because I had placed myself in a situation with various skill sets. I had a wonderful time at his company; I made a lot of mistakes, which I quickly learnt from, and I learnt a lot about myself. By the time I left his company, I was ready for the world of work. A lot of people I know struggled to get work because they did not have the experience, but I did not because I had managed to get some very important work experience. This would not have happened if I was not in the Risca Male Choir. Working for Paul gave me the knowledge that I needed to go out in the world and to become what I am today.

In chapter two I mentioned how I learnt about the spirit of never giving up with the rugby club. I learnt this with the choir as well. In December 2012, two other young top tenors and I were going to be performing a song together. We were to do this song for two concerts but the first night we mucked it up. We did not join in together and I forgot my lines. We had another crack at it the next night and it went perfectly well. I have the CD of that performance and I listen to it all the time. At this point I was keen to learn from every little thing that happens in the day. I had just recovered from depression so I was enjoying life and I just wanted to enjoy every single moment of life. My fiancée Suzie had just seen me recover from nearly a year of depression and there she was watching me singing away with a smile. We sang Elton John's *Electricity* from the musical *Billy Elliot* and the last words of the song are: "I am free". When I suffered from depression all I did was sing and sing and I sang my way out of depression. I was afraid of the unknown but when I got the courage to go and face the unknown I found friendships that will last forever and confidence like I had never known. In 2013 before the Christmas concert, which was to be my last, I got to the venue early and I sat on the stage before everyone else arrived. Whilst drying a few tears, I realised that it was a journey that I needed to take, then it hit me how much I had grown and how ready I was to face the world. I was sad to say goodbye but I was glad that I made the choice to face the unknown heaven because I walked in a boy who was scared of his own shadow, and I walked out a fearless young man.

In conclusion, a lot of people are not successful because they are not willing to do anything that is out of their comfort zone. They do exactly the same things they have done over the years and still expect to get different results. You have to believe that certain things were made just for you to do—not your family and friends—and walk your journey and dance to the beat of your own drum and not other's. Do not be scared of the unknown and do not put limitations on yourself because you are capable of learning everything that you need to know in your journey. Do not worry that you will not be as good as other successful people. If you become successful, it is because you are good enough. You have to believe that you have skills that other people do not. You have to have faith that you are going to make it, you have to really see by faith and not by sight; that's all I had on the day I found out I had failed high school, faith that I would graduate one day. This took me out of my comfort zone, in other words a known hell, a comfortable place. When you get up from that place, work, relationship you are not happy with and follow what you really want, you will find that unknown heaven which the majority of people are scared of going to because they are not sure what's there. In the unknown heaven you will *Arise and shine*!

Chapter 5

The Power of the Mind

When I was young I always used to observe all my older relatives and one thing that I noticed was the variation in terms of the amount of success that each of my aunties and uncles experienced. It is thought that people who are successful are lucky or had other advantages that enabled them to succeed. One of my mum's cousins who is a rabbi comes to mind. His father did not have enough money but he managed to go to university. He had to work really hard and he had to walk very long distances every day just to get to university; it was hard and a lot of the time he felt like just giving up. The question is why do you have a person from a poor family becoming successful and a person who grew up in a well-off family becoming poor?

Different answers to this question have been proposed but I believe that the one thing that matters when it comes to becoming successful or not is how we use our minds. The biggest human asset is the most under used asset that you will find: people do not put their minds to good use. What they do not realise is that the mind is the biggest tool to becoming what you want to be. People spend a lot of money on less important thing like clothes, shoes and jewellery and very little effort is made to increase the effectiveness of the mind. What a lot of people do not realise is that everything that we achieve in life begins in the mind and whatever our minds come up with we will become just that and nothing else.

Why do I think the mind is the most valuable tool that a human being has? I believe this because everything that we achieve begins in the mind. Everything that has ever been made began as an idea, an idea that popped in that person's mind. However, a lot of us have put less importance on the power that the mind has. We marvel at all the wonderful things that are being created today and we ask how people can do so much great work. We can do great work if we want to, we can let our mind go to work for us. Many people do not use their imagination at all when if we use our mind properly, it will go to work and it will enable us to see things we have not even thought could be done. All the feats in science and business have been achieved through imagination. People imagine how they would like things to be done and they go out and do things the way they think they should be done. A lot of people have nothing in their lives but imagination and a lot of people have everything in their life except imagination.

When I was growing up I remember hearing a story of how a young man took over his late father's business and managed to run it down to the ground, despite the fact that it was a very successful business. You can have the best things in life but if you do not have imagination, you will lose it all. For those who are in business, you will know that things change very quickly and you have to think about how things are going to be in the next few years. You must use your imagination to know how you are going to deal with a crisis. I think a lot of small businesses went under during the recession of 2008 because most small business owners did not use imagination in their organisation; they did not have a plan for what they would do if things went wrong. Their business was doing well, but they did not have plans to make it stronger if the wider economy went down. A man or woman with a strong mind-set will have a clearly defined plan.

So many people who lost their businesses in the period between 2008 and 2012 have not gone back into business at all. A person with a strong mind-set and a strong imagination would have bounced back straight away and those with a lack of imagination have stayed down. You can be 10 feet tall but if you do not have a strong imagination, you will amount to nothing.

Earl Nightingale once said that "the trouble with man today is that man does think at all". I think this idea sums up why a lot of people are not successful. Everything you will accomplish in your life begins with a thought. Everything that man has ever made was because of a thought that was put to good use. When I was about eighteen years old I had a lot of time to think about what was happing in my life on any given day. However, when I was in university, technological advances had made it very difficult to go to this place where I could think. This is true for a lot of young people today; there are just a lot of things that keep them occupied so much so they cannot get away from their friends or have some quality 'me time'. A lot of people do not realise how detrimental this can be to their health; remember that for you to do everything you were born to do, you have to be healthy. The amount of young people who go to school or employment on about two to four hours of sleep is growing year by year. There is always a new product or game on the market to keep everyone up all night.

You will not be able to think properly if you are not giving your mind a proper rest. You are not able to look back at the end of the day and analyse the day's events and discover what you are really good at. The truth is, a lot of people go through life never knowing what their biggest strengths are and, in the end, they tend to do everything apart from that one thing that they were born to do. You have to ensure that you make time to reflect on your strengths and how you are going to use them to help you create a you that you want.

Taking time to think is important because you will reflect on what you want to be and how to become what you want to be. A lot of people go through life in a manner that suggests that they cannot change their destiny at all. I had a friend who got married very young. He was about eighteen years old at the time and the marriage did not last and it did not surprise us at all. I have not seen my friend for a couple of years or more, but the effects of the decision at a very young age are still with him. He has not moved on in life. He once had a dream to go to university which he gave up to marry an older woman. We are born with a brain and a lot of us just refuse to use it; we refuse to reflect on the impact of our decisions. If we take time to think, our mind will give us all the possibilities for the future.

I remember when my friend met this woman, everything moved so fast it was unreal. I remember talking to him when they first started going out; the next time I saw them they were engaged; a few weeks later they had set the date for the wedding. We were all really caught off guard by this; it was all set; our friend was getting married and we all knew it was going to be a big mistake. I remember all the times I saw him after the announcement of the wedding. I was like, "what are you doing to yourself?" I think my friend made the decision to marry this woman because things just seemed to be too good to be true and looking back now it was too good to be true. I remember having to do a lot of thinking before asking my better half to marry me. I had to think about what the future meant for me. I advise everyone to make time to think about what you are going through and see if it has a future or not. If it has a future, hold on to it; if there is no future whatsoever in what you are doing, it's time to throw it away. You will only be able to do this if you spend time to think and reflect and stop reacting in the moment.

A lot of us react in the moment and this is because we do not spend time thinking and reflecting on every aspect of our lives. Using our mind to think will make us better people and we will stop reacting and start acting. A lot of us have spent years reacting to things that have happened to us in the past and we are not acting on opportunities that are right in front of us. I spoke about my friend Libby, she did not just react to what was going on in that moment when she found out she might not become a teacher after all; she looked at what was out there for her and what she could do to continue supporting her precious little girl. This is called the power of thinking. I think this is the most underutilised aspect of living; people have not mastered the use of their mind at all. If people decide to use their mind they will be successful. For any person to achieve great heights in life they have to use their biggest asset which is their mind, however, a lot of people do not use their mind, they just react to what is going on without giving it as much as a thought. If we decided not to think, we would not be able to realise the great possibilities that are there for us. A lot of people wake up every morning not knowing where they are going because they just cannot see the possibilities that are out there for them because they cannot use their mind. A lot of people do not realise the power their minds have to change the future, everything that you will ever do and achieve will come from the mind.

Have you ever started a journey without knowing where you are going? I think everyone will know the answer to this question. Whenever you are going on the journey you need to make a clear plan of where you are going, where you are going to make a stopover to have some food and what time you expect to get to your destination. When you get up on a Saturday morning, you know what shop you are going to and what food you are going to buy. Everything that we do in our daily lives has a goal associated with it but a lot of people for some reason do not have a goal in their lives. Can you imagine if you just woke up one morning and started driving your car not knowing where you are going – it would be a waste of petrol and your time. You have to have a goal in life because then you will know where you are going. The mind won't go to work for you because you are still in the car park without a plan of where you want to go. This means you will remain where you are and you will not move forward at all. If you are not happy with where you are in life, the first thing that you have to do is sit down and write down a goal. You have to have a goal and review it every day; you must keep it ingrained in your mind.

Having a goal of going to university kept me going even when I had depression. The fact that the goal was well and truly ingrained in me meant I was not going to give up. I wondered how I was going to do it but the goal was there even though I was down but I was not out because I was looking toward the goal every day. Look at the goal each and every day and your mind will not look at what is going wrong around you or what you cannot do. It will instead tell you what you are good at. The fact is that the only thing that will be in your mind is your goal; answers will be given to you when the time is right.

Some people want the answers to life straight away. Well, I have some bad news for you: you will not get the answers to life by just sitting on your sofa watching television; you will get the answers by having a clearly defined goal. You must know what you really want to be and what you want to do. You have to sit down and make a plan in your mind of how you are going to get there. This is the only way you are going to start your journey to success. You must remember that success is the progressive realisation of worthy ideals as defined by the great Earl Nightingale. I think this the best definition of success that I have come across from all the reading and research I have done. I therefore decided I was going to use this definition in this book. From this definition, we can ascertain that a goal is anything that will make our lives worth living. If we do not have goals in life, we will not enjoy our lives as much as we want to or as much as we should. You have to ensure that you keep your eyes on the goal and nothing else. When things are not going as well as they should, you must make sure that you make time to really look at your goal and really define it.

If you have a clearly defined goal, you will know that there are obstacles but you will be able to overcome those obstacles. Thinking about your goal will keep you believing that all things are possible; remember all things are possible, nothing is impossible and even the word itself says 'I'm possible.' You can do everything you want to do only if you have a clear defined goal you are heading to.

A lot of people do not make any time in their life to think, this is because they do not have a goal they are working towards. As a result, they spend their time doing things that will not make them grow. Growth begins in the mind and giving time to thinking. A lot of people reach a certain age and it's almost like how on earth have I got here? It's almost like their life is one massive accident, however, it is not, and they are surprised with where they are in their life through not planning. Now, how much time do we spend on self-development? The maximum working hours in the United Kingdom is about forty hours a week that leaves you with about 72 hours when we are neither sleeping nor working. Most people spend this time doing things that will not make them grow; they go through life day by day without picking up any lessons at all. An example of this is a person who has had a long day, gets home, has a shower, has some dinner and spends the rest of the evening watching television. Their partner realises they are still downstairs, goes down and tells them to switch the television off. They do this every night and wonder why they are so tired in work all the time. Tiredness means you miss those little details that makes you an excellent worker. What do you think will become of this person in a few decades to come? I presume they will probably be at the same level in their job or would have moved from one job to the other because they are tired of seeing new people coming into the business and getting promoted when they have been there for a long time.

What they don't realise is that they are not progressing in their career because they are not progressing in their mind; it all begins in the mind. I found a quote on the internet by the legendary George Bernard Shaw which said: "I became successful by thinking two days a week, the trouble with a lot of people is that they do not think at all." I think that is the trouble with a lot of people today, they are either watching television or talking to friends on social media so much so they have no time for 'me time' to think and reflect and rest properly for the mind to be clear and capable of thinking constructively in the morning.

You have to spend time writing down your ideas and plans for the future, this will give you more control over your life. You will act on things and people and not react to people, which a lot of people do. If you do not have enough rest, you will probably be a person who reacts to everything in your life because your mind will be just too tired to think constructively. I would suggest after you finish school, university or work you spend time when you get home to think. This will help you to know where you are in your life and how near you are to your dreams or how many opportunities you have in your life. Many people who are gifted do not even know that they are gifted because they do not spend time thinking and reflecting on the things that they do. You have to make time to count your blessings, which is a very difficult thing to do when things are not going well. My priest once said the most difficult arithmetic to do is the one that enables you to count your blessings. A lot of people cannot count their blessing only because they do not have time to think of who they are and what they have and what they are really capable of doing. You have to take time to think of what is going on in your life and look at your own abilities and try and find out what skills your company needs. That progressive realisation we spoke about will only come about if you make time to actually realise it.

In your 72 hours you have free, you can spend that time thinking about what you want and I also advise that you make time to read and listen to motivational material. If you are going to spend a lot of time on YouTube, you might as well spend it listening to the greatest thinkers that ever lived. I listen to the great Zig Ziglar, Napoleon Hill, Les Brown and the majestic Earl Nightingale then I say a little prayer to thank the Lord for the day. No matter how bad it was, I am thankful that I am alive. Feed your mind then go and have some leisure time and what you are thinking about will come to you because your subconscious mind will go to work for you). Do not waste your time not becoming anything; you were born to win but you can only win if you use your mind wisely. You can only win if you spend time feeding your mind the right stuff; you can only win if you spend time studying and reviewing your dream each and every day.

We have now established that we become what we think about and that the only way we are going to be really successful in life is if we have the right things in our minds. When I was in high school a lot of people told me that I was not good at anything and so I acted like I was not good at anything. This was what was going on in my mind. I currently commute from Gloucester to Bristol five days a week and I can read through a lot of things on my journey. I realised that my mood for that day was being affected by what I was reading on my journey so I started reading and listening to inspirational material on my journey and my mood for the day improved. Certain thoughts have been put in our minds since childhood and we can only change this if we start feeding our mind with the right stuff. Everything that you have accomplished so far is a result of what you have been feeding your mind. I suggest that if you really want to *Arise and Shine*, you have to change what goes into our minds. A lot of people do not realise that their lives are being shaped by what they allow into their minds.

People who are successful have allowed all the right things to go into their minds. They have read books that inspire them and tell them that the word impossible does not exist. Before something is accomplished, everyone thinks it is impossible until someone else does that very thing. You have to really make sure that you deliberately make time to put great things in your mind, things that will tell you that nothing is really impossible in this world. You will never *Arise and Shine* if all you put in your mind are things that tell you nothing can be done or you are not good enough. Remember that we become what we think about and if all you are putting in your mind are things that tell you that you are not good enough, you will think and then really believe that you are not good enough. Once you convince yourself that you are not good enough, you will set your bars really low and you will hit them.

You will become like a lot of people who go from one job to the other and never aim to do anything that will challenge them. They will aim to do what they think they can do and will not go for anything that they do not know how to do it.

Zig Ziglar once said that we are all where we are and what we are because of what we feed our minds. We are all where we are at this point in time because of what we have been putting in our minds and we can change were we are and what we are by changing what goes in our minds. The mind can be compared to a plot of land; it will not tell you what you should build or plant on it. You decide what you are going to do with it as the owner. This is the same with the mind; we decide what we put in the mind and what we put in the mind is what it produces. Let's say a farmer buys a plot of land and he plants apple trees on it; the only fruit he will get is apples and nothing else. We are where we are because of the seed that we have planted in our own minds. We are not doing well in work or school because we have planted a seed that is not good enough and we are bearing the fruits that we planted. This is the main reason I said that we should make time to reflect on what is going into our minds and try and see if it is affecting our progress in life.

You will only progress in life if you change your thoughts from negative to positive. We should evaluate what sort of people we spend most of our time with; are they the people who will encourage us to live our dream or are they the people that tell us all our flaws including those we did not know existed? My friend who wanted to be a fashion designer listened to what people told her and she did not become a fashion designer because that was what her mind had been fed. We should try and spend time with people who will encourage us to grow and think big. You can be whatever you want to be: all you need to do is feed your mind with the right things. I became a loner in my BTEC year because I just got really tired of people in my class saying we were a class full of people who would amount to nothing. I refused to listen to this and I refused to spend time with them.

I had a dream and I thought it was possible even though other people thought this was not the case. The previous academic year I was the kid who had failed his exams and now here I was with a dream of going to university in the next three years. You can change where you are and what you are by changing what goes in your mind. I stopped listening to what other people were saying about me and started listening to myself; whatever your dreams, never let other people's opinion of you become your reality.

You may look at what you have achieved so far in your life compared to other people and think you are just not good enough. This is not the case, just look at what you have been feeding your mind most of your life and remember you can change where you are and what you are by changing what goes in your mind. It sounds too simple to be true, but it is true that we become what we think about. So, what do we think about? We think about all the things that we are putting in our minds; if we change what we put in our minds, we will change what we think about. The day I failed my exam a great thing happened, my thoughts were transformed in what felt like a twinkling of an eye; a seed was planted and my thoughts were changed for the better.

'Come on Frank, that is just too easy!' Yes, it is that easy to change your thoughts and change your life. One of my favourite verses in the bible says: "Be ye transformed by the renewing of your mind." You can be transformed the moment you decide you are going to become the person you want to be. You will never blame circumstances at all because you will know that you have the power to change whatever you are going through. May I just point out that a lot of people are running around like headless chickens with no goals to work towards, hence they cannot change what goes in their mind. You have to set a goal in your life for your mind to start taking away all the negative thoughts that you have been putting in for a number of years. If you have never set a goal, set yourself a short-term goal and work towards that. The relief I got from passing my A levels was tremendous, I was going to university. I had achieved my first major goal in life by putting positive things in my mind. Start today by reading and listening to positive material, you will get to hear stories of people who were worse off compared to you; people who have changed their lives for the better. Do not worry where you are, you can move forward by changing what goes in your mind.

One of the most important aspects of living a successful life is finding time to offload your mind at the end of the day. The understanding that some days are going to be better than others will serve very well in life. When you get home, you should find time to offload all the bad things that might have been in your mind. It is important that you do this because we become what we think about and if we do not take time to empty our minds of all the bad things that might have happened in the day, before we know it we will be carrying all the things that have not worked out for us and our outlook on life will be different. One of the things I had to do when I decided I was going to go to university was to empty my mind at the end of the day. I had to do this because I was learning about myself; I was not great because I was only getting started on my journey. The greatest mistake that a lot of people make is to focus on the things that they are not good at and neglect the things they are good at. I suggest that after a very bad day you go home and spend an hour or so emptying your mind. You will never grow as a person if you are carrying negative things in your mind.

I think one of the worst things people do is listening to the news just before they go to bed. We know that the only thing that is in the news today is bad news. If you had an awful day at work and you get home and put your television set on and listen to the news then all you are putting in your mind is bad news. A terrible day at work plus listening to bad news will not make you grow as a person. You will be anxious most of your day and this will stop you from thinking through everything you do. We have to make a mind filter that will allow only the things that will make us grow to stay in the mind and stop those that will lead us to a life of anger and unhappiness.

One day I had a very bad day at work and when I got home I was still angry about the events of that day. I was so angry I could not sleep. I managed only a few hours' sleep and when I got out of bed I was still angry. To top it off because of the lack of sleep I was not in a good mood and events of the previous day made me even more angry. I had the worst day one can have; I was arguing with people all day long, I was short with everyone. Everything that I did on that particular day was a result of the previous day's events. From then on, I decided that every time I go home I would go and empty my mind completely of all the things that went wrong on that day. When I do this, I find that I rest very well and when I wake up the following morning I am able to say that it is a brand-new day. A brand-new day means a brand-new page to start over again. Remember, we are where we are and what we are because of what goes into our minds, so if we get up in the morning with an attitude that will allow our minds to go to work for us, it will. We must really watch what we are allowing into our minds each and every day.

A lot of us will take care of our clothes, our houses and our cars better than our own minds. We protect all the things that have a price tag but we forget the thing that is priceless. A lot of us go through a week of work and when we get home we just think it is the weekend, time to do everything we can do when we are not working. We forget to reflect on our skills and all the good things that are going well for us in our current job. When we reflect about our jobs, we focus only on the bad things that happened in work during the week. When we do this, we overlook all the opportunities that we have each and every day that we would notice if we only put positive thoughts in our mind. At the end of that day go home and reflect on all the good things you like about your boss and your work, look at what you are learning and what you need to learn and what you have learnt and then completely empty your mind of all the things you were not happy with or did not do well during the course of the day. Some days are always going to be better than others, but while you are in the darkness of night remember that a new day is about to dawn.

I have said in this chapter many times that where we are and what we are is because of what goes into our minds. Many people look for the negatives in everything so what if *you* programmed *your* mind to look for the positives in everything? One of my friends went for a job interview and when he came out of it, even though he did not get the job, he was thinking about all the good things that came out of it. Experience is a very good teacher; however, do not let experience determine your destiny. You have to reflect on all the good things that came out of the experience and count your blessings. Think of positive things like the joy of being alive and having all these opportunities. You should always tell yourself that things are working out for the best. When I failed my exams, I could have told myself that nothing would ever work out for me, instead I told myself that I was going to go to university. I did not do what a lot of people do after failing an exam, sitting down and feeling sorry for myself for the rest of my adult life. I was not doing very well in high school but from the 23rd August I started telling myself I could do this.

The kid who had low self-esteem and no goals in life was now a dreamer with a great desire to achieve what he was dreaming about. A lot people fail in life not because they failed in the past, but rather it is because they miss all the opportunities that the present day puts in front of them. You have to empty your mind of all the negative things that have gone on in your past and focus on what today and tomorrow will bring. It is important you look at what you have planted in your mind. Like I said earlier, whatever you plant in your mind will become productive; whatever we have achieved in our life this far, we are just reaping what we have sowed.

How can we change our mindsets and actually *Arise and Shine*? When I started primary school, I was really slow compared to all the kids my age in class. When my year one teacher saw that I was struggling, all she did was to encourage the class to make fun of me. My class had a song for me and it went like this: "Mr Bean is a fool, Mr Bean is mad". This was the song that most people in my year sang whenever they saw me. Here I was a six-year-old kid just starting out in life with a lot to learn and here was a teacher who was tearing me apart before I even started. It was a very bad start; I was never going to be the popular kid in school. I struggled through my first two years and when I went to year three I had to be taken back a year. When I went down a year that's when I realised that little year one song was a well-known song around the school. I remember walking round the school grounds and this kid I had never seen before went past me singing, "Saliki Chama is a fool, Mr Bean is mad" (I was called Saliki Chama in primary school even though I was registered as Frank Chama Saliki). I was heartbroken to hear random kids singing this song to me, I thought I was not as special as the other young kids. Children are all special and it is just that the world wants to make certain kids not feel special. I carried all this in my subconscious mind and when my conscious mind thought I was not good enough, the subconscious mind showed me the evidence to that thought. As a result, as I grew up and wherever I went, I thought I was not good enough.

This was not true. My first-year teacher did not give me a chance and when I had a chance to prove I was good enough, I passed with flying colours. And when I was in year six, I was in a special class (in Zambia a special class was a class where all the high achievers were and I was one of the top students in some subjects). Remember that we become what we think about; we can change where we are and what we are by changing what we put in our minds. I went from a year one pupil who was mocked by everyone to a year six pupil who was one of the top students in the top class in school. I went from a high school failure to a university graduate in six years. All this happened because I started thinking that I could do it and my subconscious mind gave the evidence I needed to really believe that I could. One of the things that helped me was looking back at times that I did very well and reliving those moments over and over again. From August 2007 success was the only word in my head; I have become what I thought about and since I thought success, I became successful. You should make sure that you think success and abundance because if you do, you will achieve success in abundance.

The power of the mind determines whether we are going to be successful or not in what we are doing. The questions here is: do people have the power to control their mind? I think the answer to this question is yes. You see, when a garden is watered and fertilised all the things in the garden will flourish; you will have a nice green garden and only the things you want will grow. If you stop tending your garden, all the things that you do not want in it will grow. My fiancée and I just recently

111

bought a new house and the garden was untidy; the grass had grown very long and there were a lot of plants growing we did not particularly want.

The mind can be compared to a garden because when we stop putting positive things into your mind, all the negatives will start to grow. You see, to keep a lovely green garden requires a lot of work while a garden full of weeds requires no effort at all. This means that to keep a positive mind you have to keep working all the time without fail. William James, the American philosopher once said: "you can change your life by changing your attitude of mind." Whatever we do all begins in the mind and in order to be successful you will have to look at weeds you have kept in your mind all these years that you really need to pull out and replace them with beautiful roses. A lot of people are not successful because they keep holding on to things they really do not want; they carry them with every day in their mind. Since we become what we think about, they fail at everything they do because they are constantly thinking of failure. When they are about to embark on anything unfamiliar, they always ask themselves what happens if they fail and never what if I really make it.

A few people have said to me that it is not very easy to move from being a negative thinker to a positive thinker. I don't think it is true. It is very easy to change your state of mind and get what you want in life, it means simply changing what we put in our minds. A lot of people try to change their lives without changing their attitude of mind. The fact that we become what we think about means that we will never be successful if we are thinking we are going to fail any time we do anything new. We will fail in things we are really good at if we think we are going to fail. To be successful we have to practise thought replacement, which means replacing negative thoughts with positive thoughts. You know that nice garden you have in your house will only become a glorious garden if you replace the weeds with the colourful flowers you want. You can change your mind by replacing your unwanted thoughts with ones you want. You must actively be involved in becoming a positive thinker, which a lot of people do not do. You may just end up ticking all negative attitudes that a lot of people have. One of the things I did when I decided to go to university was take out all the things that had been holding me back. After being bullied throughout my school years, I added these events together and I came up with: "Frank you are not good enough."

Throughout high school I had thought I was not good enough and I was not going to amount to anything. This thought kept going through my mind until that day in August when I decided that I had a purpose: I was going to go to university and I was going to graduate. I made up my mind, I was going to make it. I started spending time to disprove what I was told in the past by putting positive thoughts in my mind. I was a kid without a plan, without a dream, but now I had a dream and I had a plan and I was going to make it. You know why? It's because I *thought* I would make it.

One of the things that a lot of people do not do is take action towards the things that they are scared of. You have to take action to overcome your fears; if you think you are not be able to do something and you do not do it, you will spend the rest of your life thinking you cannot do it. If you have a go, you might just discover that you can. If you do this, it will take charge of your mind. I believe that the moment I decided I was going to go to university I became a totally new person. I changed my attitude of mind. I still struggled in a lot of ways but because I had an 'I will' attitude, I learnt a lot of things quicker than I did before. Even if I struggled in anything, I knew that all I needed to do was to study more in that subject. As a result, I got better at a lot of subjects doing things this way. When we think we are on the wrong path in life, why do we still stay on that road? A lot of people know that their way of thinking is wrong but they still stay on that road when they have an opportunity to change by simply changing what goes into their minds. I believe that a lot of people do not even realise that they are living a life that has been scripted by other people. Imagine starting a book and someone else completes it for you, you will be looking at the book and saying, "that is not what I wanted to do with that character," or, "I had bigger dreams for that character." Imagine you are a character in a book: think of the things you want to do with that character. Write down the ending you want for that character: do you want to see them fail in life or be successful? Think of all the things you want to see that character achieve, imagine seeing them rising from glory to glory. You see a lot of people see themselves falling and falling. The book of Romans says: "Be ye transformed by the renewing of your mind!" You can change where you are and what you are by changing what goes into your mind.

Every morning when I get up I always ensure that I read or listen to something positive. The subconscious mind is very impressionable first thing in the morning, whatever you put in your mind will determine what your day is going to be like. I started doing this when I discovered that my mood would change depending on if I heard bad news on the TV or good news, so I decided to just listen to good news every morning. This has proved very effective for the last three months; I think more positively about everything I am doing and I love my job a lot more using this method. I always make sure that I put the good, the positive, the pure and the powerful into my mind. I do this because I do not want to be a wondering generality when I can easily become a meaningful specific.

I believe that a lot of people do not do well in life because they are always putting negative things in their minds. They will tell you everything that is wrong in the world. It is almost like the whole world does not want to hear about anything good that is going on in the world. I think the world is not as perfect as we would like it to be, but I still believe that there are as many good things as bad things going on and I want to believe that it is generally a good place to live in. One of the things I do before I go to sleep is listen to great speakers like Earl Nightingale, Zig Ziglar, Tony Robbins and Les Brown. This way the last thing I think about before going to bed is something positive because, just like in the morning, the subconscious mind is very impression-able when you are sleeping. The last thing you thought about is stored in there, hence why you wake up angry if the last thing you did was argue with somebody the night before. You have to make sure that you empty your mind of all the bad things by replacing them with good thoughts. This will mean that when you wake up in the morning you will be thinking about something that will make you grow and think better about life and other people. Even if I have had a bad day, I find that listening to positive thoughts at the end of the day makes my day becomes a great day and I am truly thankful for it. Doing this will make you forget all the negative things from that day and every day will be worthwhile. You must always remember that you can only achieve if you think you can.

To conclude this chapter, you must always remember that your mind is like a field and whatever you plant in it will grow accordingly. We are where we are and what we are because of what goes into our minds and we can change by changing what goes into our mind. A lot of people are not successful in life because they do not have a plan of where they want to be; they have no direction or goals in life. You can only achieve things in life if you have a clear and defined goal in your mind. Only then will you be successful. Be transformed by the renewing of your mind. In order for you to change your life you must change your way of thinking. So long as you think negatively about yourself, you will not be successful because we become what we think about. Everything that you have achieved in your life so far is as a result of your own personal belief, and if you change your beliefs, you will change where you are in your life. In other words, think the right thoughts about yourself and take action to change the way your subconscious mind thinks and really convince yourself that you were born to win. The mind should not have power over us; we should control our mind, we have the power. If we control what goes into our minds and only allow positive things to go in we shall surely *Arise and Shine*!

Chapter 6

Stay In Control

On my way to work one day I heard two women talking on the train. One of them said that you must make sure to try and stay calm, like water deep down in the sea. I thought this was a very strange thing to say. I was thinking about this for the whole day in work. I went home and did some research on this and I found out what this woman had meant and it was very sound advice. You see, when the waves are throwing everything about on top of the sea, the water deep down stays still. It is not affected by what is going on above. A lot of people let what is happening on the surface affect them. What a lot of people do not realise is that life is ten percent what happens to you and ninety percent how you respond to what happens to you. When I failed my high school exams, I could have done what a lot of people who have failed exams have done – become completely defeated and give up on their life at an early age. That is too early to give up on living a very happy life. The day I failed my exam, an inner calmness like no other was born. I stopped looking at what was happening on the surface and looked deep in the water to see what the reality was. A lot of people just look at the surface and they see everything going wrong but if they were to look deeper, they would see the calmness to help go through life in joy or in sorrow. You must ensure that you always look deeper because you can only see as deep as you look. The wind and the waves will throw you here and there, but if you stay in charge and in control of yourself, you will overcome all your trials and tribulations. Those people who only look at what is on the surface will never make it in life; every time they run into difficulties they will quit and – you have heard it been said before: quitters never win. These people look for an easy life and when things start going wrong they put their tools down and wait for a miracle to happen. Miracles only happen if you take actions to overcome the difficulty you are going through.

There was a competition in the USA to see who could come up with a picture that best represented peace. A lot of wonderful drawings were submitted such as wonderful summer mornings with green grass and beautiful colours. This is what people think peace is, as one well-known hymns goes: 'all things bright and beautiful.' However, the drawing that won was one depicting really heavy rain, wind blowing everything all over the place, and, in the right hand corner of the picture, a bird looking after her little ones there in the nest on the cleft of the rock, calm and collected. I think that's what peace is all about. A lot of people say they will have peace once they are happy. They go out there chasing happiness, but what they do not realise is that you are only going to be happy once you have peace. You see dear friend, happiness is a state of being; you have to be peaceful with yourself to love yourself for who you are and stop comparing yourself to other people. Your mind can only work very well if you have deep inner peace. When I was studying to go to university, I started waking up at four in the morning because it was calm and peaceful and I could think clearly. If you have peace within yourself, nothing will stop you. You will be able to use the great engine of the mind you possess, and you will power through your entire problem with ease. I was thinking to myself when I was singing that famous hymn in church 'It Is Well With My Soul' – is it really well with my soul? If it is truly well with your soul, you will stay still and you will overcome.

When I was thinking of staying in control, I thought of a university graduate who did really well in his exam and wanted to get the best job out there. There was only one problem: it was after the recession and graduate jobs were few and far between. He managed to get a simple admin job, which he hated, and I remember him saying: "I have a first-class honours degree and I am doing this stupid admin job." He had a plan for his life and now it was not going the way he wanted. The most difficult arithmetic to do is the one that enables you to count your blessing. He thought he deserved better and never saw the opportunity that he had in front of him. The job market was really difficult for a graduate, but he never saw it as an opportunity. The last time I saw him he was going to work in his local corner shop. He has not gained any experience so he is not considered for all the jobs he applies for. I remember him saying that he wondered why he did not get a job and how opportunities were not coming his way at all. He has found himself in this situation just because he refused to look at the job he got as an opportunity to get started.

He forgot one thing: you have to start from the bottom before you get to the top. You might be at the bottom now but look at your attitude towards your job: do you do it with joy? Before you can even think about getting promoted in your current job, you have to be really good at it. It might not be what you wanted it to be, but you must ensure that you stay in control and do the job very well.

I work with a lot of people who are older than me and I can tell why they are not at the top or enjoying their lives. They are always complaining and they do just enough to stop themselves from getting fired. I think the people who make it in life are those who are willing to do more than they are paid for. I remember going into work and this older co-worker telling me that I did not have to do what I was doing because I was not paid enough to carry on doing that. Now this is an attitude of a person you will never see at the top.

In August 2014 I started working at one of the Hospitals in Bristol and I found that people at the bottom of any organisation do not really help each other at all. One day, one of the most difficult patients I had faced in my job had something to complain about and I went to cover another ward in the afternoon. The patient came to the desk and my colleague decided she did not want to deal with them so she said she did not know what was going on. I think if I had been working with really successful people, they would have picked that issue up and dealt with it because that's what successful people do.

Society has changed so much over the last decade or so, people are more focussed on what they get in life and not what other people will get in life. The fact that the human race is very quickly moving away from helping each other has resulted in a lot of people not having what they want in life. You see to be successful in life you need people. When I was in my last year of university, I was looking for an internship but I could not find one at all until a man I sung with in a male voice choir told me he was a Human Resources Manager and offered me a job. What a lot of people have forgotten is that we need other people to be successful in life and if we do not do this, we will fail. If you want to create a better world, it must firstly start with you. A lot of people will tell you about how the world is such a bad place these days and they will not be the first people to lend a helping hand. However, they expect other people to help them when they are in need. I discovered a beautiful Christian hymn called *A Beautiful Life* and the chorus of the song says, 'Each day I will do a golden deed by helping those who are in need.' I believe that for the human race to stay in control they will have to be helpful to one another; remember you can only like other people for who they are if you like yourself for who you are.

Zig Ziglar, in his speech 'See You At The Top', said you must help other people get what they want and you will get what you want. I thought that this was very strange thing to say, but the more I thought about it, the more it made sense. Many people have set up businesses and failed in the first few months because they believe that all they have to do is to make money. They focus on getting customers to come to their business and spend money and they give them the product and nothing else. You see people will only return to the business if they feel the business cares about their needs. It is important that we understand that unless we give other people what they want, we will not get what we want. One day my friend came from work and he was very disgruntled about his boss. He was talking about how much he hated him and he was not going to work two minutes more than he is paid for. He was not going to give his boss any more time. Then, when a promotion came up, a person who had only been in the company for a few months got the job. The next time I saw him he was angry like I had never seen him before and he talked about how his boss did not value his work. The truth is that he did not have enough control in him to help other people get what they wanted. His boss helped his colleague get what he wanted only because my friend had not helped his boss get what he wanted. He worked in an organisation longer than most people but he did not get the recognition he thought he deserved because he only did the job he was paid to do and no more. There is an old saying that you reap what you sow; if you want people to do you favours in life, you must first of all sow the seed by helping others reap what they want. No matter how bad things might be going, you must make sure that you help other people get what they want.

There was a lady I was acquainted with at university. I didn't know her very well but the one thing I knew was that she was a really kind person; she was always there to help other people. I remember one lady saying that she had run out of food and this lady had helped her by sharing what little she had. A lot of us think we have to have a lot to share, but keeping in control means sharing what little we have with other people who do not have anything. I once overheard her say that she still has biscuits in the cupboard for visitors when she has nothing for herself. This was a woman with so much love for other people. She was willing to help other people all the time. She did it with love but what she never realised was that she was sowing a seed of success and she was going to reap that success in the few years ahead. When we graduated from university and were on the hunt for jobs, we went looking but she did not have to. She had sowed the seed and all she had to do then was reap. You see, one of the people she helped has a brother who owned a business and he asked him to take this lady as well.

So you see, she had helped someone get what they wanted, and when she needed a job the same person that she had helped then helped her get that job. She did not have to go searching; she went from our last exam into full-time employment. You will truly only get what you want by helping other people get what they want. You must make sure that you keep planting and watering that seed and one day, in a very unexpected way, you shall reap the fruits of your labour; just make sure you labour and never rest from labouring and you are going to get what you want in your life. But only if you help enough other people get what they want. I think that is why the lord Jesus said: "Love your neighbour as you love yourself," because those you help will be there for you when you least expect them to be.

Another thing I noticed was she never judged other people, she looked at everyone as if they were wonderfully made. As a Christian, I believe that God made all of us wonderfully. If all you do in your life is judge other people, you will not achieve anything in life. Many people have missed opportunities in life because they just judged other people too quickly. I found that out when the man I sang with in a male voice choir, who turned out to be a HR manager of the company he worked for; he helped me get what I was looking for. I can confess I never thought he held such a position, but he did. If I had not been polite to him when I joined the choir, he would not have helped me to find what I was looking for.

In the previous chapter I spoke about being in charge of our thoughts. A lot of people are where they are in life because of the negative thoughts about other people as well as themselves. Because of this they will never help other people. They always think that it is not their responsibility, they are where they are because of themselves. What they don't realise is that the more people they help, the more friends they will make on the way. Life is a lot easier if you have a lot of friends.

I believe that to stay in control you have to have a lot of friends who are able to support you on your journey, otherwise it will get really lonely. If you decide not to help enough other people get what they want, you will also end up not getting what you want and you definitely will lose control of a happy life. One example that has stayed with me was when my friend's father got really ill, we all knew he was dying, no question. We were about 12 but we all knew what was coming. The mother collected the dad's savings and they were spending a lot of money; it was crazy I had not seen anything like it before. It was at the time when our local mining company was closed which meant the majority of people in the town had no money at all. Here was this family with a silly amount of money, buying everything they wanted. We went to school on an empty stomach while they had a lot of food. I remember them throwing food away when we did not have food at all. They never shared anything. I remember when their father passed away, their mother did not work so they had nothing. They did not get a lot of people who were willing to help them because they had not helped anybody else. They had to sell their home and the last I heard the whole family was living with their grandfather. I am reminded of an old saying which goes like this, 'Make sure you help others while you are on top because you might just need these people to get you back up when you are on the way down.' I truly believe that if they had helped more people when they had a lot of money, they would have got a lot of help. The trouble is they thought that the only way they could stay in control was to just help themselves but they ended up losing control of their lives instead.

The other way that will enable you to stay in control of your life is by feeding your mind the right things. We are where we are and what we are because of what goes into our minds; we can change this by changing what goes into our minds. A lot of people do not realise that the things they put in their minds each and every day will determine where they end up in life. One thing I do is listen to motivational things at the start of the day and at the end of the day. You see a lot of things happen in the day and we pick up a lot of things without knowing. These little things will determine where we end up in life. I suggest that every morning when you wake up you think of good things that are happening in your life, think about how blessed you are to have your family and your other half, think how blessed you are to have your job even if you do not like it. At the end of the day you must spend another ten minutes reflecting on the good things that happened during the day. I find that this helps to relax and I go to bed happy, and when I get up in the morning I feel rested and without any anxiety. A lot of people go home and they talk about everything that went wrong during the day and they go to bed thinking about who annoyed them in work. At the end of every shift I step outside, take in the fresh air, and, no matter how bad the day was, I say what a lovely evening it is. I thank the Lord that I have this ability to completely start thinking about something different at the end of the day. No matter how bad the day is, I will not be miserable when I get home. I believe that people in my life should not have a bad evening just because I had a bad day at work. It is an opportunity to enjoy what is left of the day and turn a very bad day into a day to remember. I know a lot of people argue with their partners just because work is not going well.

One thing I learnt to master when I decided I was going to go to university, even though I was a high school failure, was to live one day at a time. If I had a bad day, I would just look forward to the next day. I understood that I couldn't change yesterday, but I can change tomorrow. To stay in control of your life you have to learn from the mistakes of the day and completely move on because what you did yesterday will not determine where you end up in life, but what you do today will determine where you are going to be tomorrow. You should forget what happened in the past and focus on the gift of life you have today and look forward to what tomorrow is going to bring. A lot of people are either thinking about what happened to them in the past or worrying about what may or may not happen tomorrow. This is speculative; they get themselves worked up for no reason at all. They might just be speculating, but they do not realise that they are putting their mind to work on negative things. They will have sleepless nights worrying about something that may never happen at all. So, all you are doing is worrying about things that will never happen. By doing this they take away their peace and miss out on living a happy life. It is important that you have goals in life but the biggest mistake people make is worrying about how they are going to reach that goal when things are not good.

A lot of people focus on the difficulty of reaching that goal hence they end up giving up. They do not understand that every day is an opportunity to reach your goal. Don't focus on the difficulties because, by doing what you are supposed to be doing when you are working on your dreams, things will fall place for you. In my first year at university I had to re-sit an accounts exam but I was not very confident I had done enough. The day before the exam I was in the university library making the last touches in preparation and this lady I knew very well ended up being in the library when she was not supposed to be there. She showed me the easiest way I was meant to do it and I got it and I passed my exam. Do not look at how you are going to get there even when there are obstacles all around you, just start moving and you will make it when the time is right.

The other way to stay in control is by not listening to people who are not aiming high in their lives but by listening to people who have made it. Les Brown said: "A lot of people fail in life not because they set their bars too high and miss but it's because they set their bars too low and hit". If people who are not doing anything great in their lives tell you that a certain thing cannot be done, do not listen to them, you must listen to people who are telling you that it is possible." We were all born to win but a lot of people do not realise this, hence they settle for something less in life. Do not focus on what you are not good at, instead focus on what you are good at. Do not be like a maths genius who focuses on drama because they are not good at it and loses the gift they are born with. So many people spend all their lives trying to do things other people are good at and not what they themselves are good at, and, in the end, they end up not being good at anything. A lot of people have become successful because they have mastered the one thing they are good at and they have done better than anyone else can.

Dr Ben Carson in his book *Think Big* said his mother told him that you can do what everyone can do, but only you can do it better. I say to you that you can do what everyone else can do but there is that one thing that only you can do better. Be who you want to be and do what you want to do when you take control of your life. I believe that too many people are not what they want to be, which is why they are so unhappy. They feed themselves with the negatives and the unclean; I say feed your mind with the good, the pure and the powerful.

I heard a story once which talked about the mind being like a battleground for two wolves. A father told his son that the only wolf that wins is the one that is being fed the most. If you are always feeding your mind negative things, you will become a very negative person. Once you become negative, you will look at everything that is wrong in the world. You will always find a reason why opportunities will not come your way before you even try that thing. I think the best way to overcome fear is to do that thing you are scared of doing. A lot of us let our fears stop us from doing what we want I life. I thought of writing a book for a very long time – I thought of writing a book when I was eighteen, but I always thought I was not good enough. I always worried what people would say if I said that I was writing a book so I kept putting it off. You must take control of your life and do what you want to do. A lot of people go through life wishing they could achieve something and years go by very quickly, it feels like everything happens in the blink of an eye.

Whatever you want to do, no matter how difficult it may seem to be, just start now. People might tell you are not great enough but if you are using the positive mind, it will tell you that you do not have to be great to get started, you have to get started to be great. You have to stop the negative side of your mind; you must starve it to death by maturing the positive side of your mind. Once you make the positive mind the dominant one, even when you have those little worries like we all do now and again, you will overcome them easily, because your positive mind will be able to show you all the things you are good at. If you are a positive thinker, you will be able to learn from your day-to-day errors and move on. You must be careful because those little negative thoughts you keep in your mind might build up to something really big. Put small positive things in your mind each day and this will grow to something much better.

You might be defeated and wondering where you are going to start. Everything might look lost and you will think you have nowhere to start in life. I say you must start where you are. When I failed my exam, I had to start somewhere. I had to start where I was, right at that point in time as a high school failure. I hear a lot of people say everything that can ever happen to someone has happened to them and they have reached the lowest any human being can go. Really? Well I think it is time to get up because you have reached the lowest point you can go: there is no other way but up! It is going to be a long road ahead, so pack a lot positive thinking and enthusiasm because that is all you are going to need. You might find yourself a little cleaning job on your way up; make sure you do it with a lot of energy and joy in your eyes. You may be the lowest person in the building, but if you do it with energy you will not be, your manager will be watching. Whatever job you are doing, do not think you are just doing it for your boss, you are also doing it for yourself. Zig Ziglar once told a story of a businessman who went to his supplier and saw a very hard-working man. He had watched this man run all over the place, and anything that needed to be done he did. He thought positively about his job all the time, even though he was the lowest of the low in the organisation. The business owner made a comment about this young man: "you see him, he will be promoted soon and do you want to know how I know that, it's because if his employer doesn't, I will." As the great George Bernard Shaw once said: the people who make it in life are those that look for opportunities they want, and if they don't exist, they make them

A lot of people are not in control of their lives because they are not creating the opportunities that they want. A lot of people look around and tell you that there is nothing here for them at all. They do not look at the needs of the people in the area they are living in because they are all focussed on what the area can give them. Remember you must help as many people get what they want and then you will get what you want. They are focussed on what the city or town will give them so much that they do not realise what is missing in the town. If their first thought was what they can give this place, they would become successful. I moved from Newport, because I thought it would be a lot easier for me to get a job elsewhere, I ended up working in Gloucester for six months before I started my current job. I look back and I think that what I only saw was a city with no hope for a bright future, but I never really thought about what I could have given the city of Newport. I think a lot of people have lost it all just because they have not looked at how they can help other people. If things are not going very well and lots of people around seem to be struggling, you must think of how you can help all these people get what they want. You must aim to be creative and find out what other people do not have. My friend Libby had to look at what the people of Newbridge did not have and that was a toy shop hence she set up 'Little Hands Play.' She is providing a product and a service and she is getting what she wants and that is earning a living. In the Bible, there is a good example of being a servant, Jesus washed his disciples' feet and said do to others like I have done to you. Be a people's servant and you will gain total control of your life.

The other way one takes control of their lives is by understanding that we are all different and will react differently in a given situation. In other words, stop expecting the whole world to be like you. My very good friend once said to me that he left his job because he was so different to everyone else. What you have to understand is that we are all made differently and we have different past experiences. I have always thought that people are too quick to judge people all the time. In my current job, I find it very interesting to hear the gossip going around. This has fascinated me because one day I see two people getting along, and as soon as one is not there the other person is gossiping about them. I sometimes sit and just think about what is wrong with man today.

I find the best way to take control of my life is not getting involved in all the chatting going on about people behind their backs. I have found that people will not like you for one reason or another and you will not know why. There was a lady I got on with very well when I started my job but we do not talk anymore. It was what I thought was a really simple misunderstanding and could be sorted out very quickly, I just assumed we all had a bad day, and the next day I would apologise and we would be fine. However, it was not that simple; my apology was not accepted and we were not friends anymore. I was always careful of what I told her and other people I work with, and now she was telling other people everything that was wrong with me. It was her opinion and I always make sure I do not make other people's opinions become a reality. Imagine if I had told her about my boss, she would have had all the ammunition to make my place untenable. The best way to stay in control is by making sure that you do not focus on talking about other people just because they are different from you. It takes a world of differences to make this a better place. Learn from other people and enjoy the relationships you will have by learning from people who are different from yourself.

There is an old saying that goes, 'Birds of a feather flock together.' I think to stay in control of your life you have to have the right people around you; people you can learn from, and people who will make you grow as a person. I always say to people that if they mix with people who are always telling them what they cannot do then maybe it is time to find another group. We are all where we are and what we are because of what goes into our minds and we can change where we are and what we are by changing what goes into our minds. If you are spending time with people who are constantly telling you what you cannot do you will be filling your mind with things you cannot do that will make you feel inadequate and, in the end, when this starts happening, you will start thinking you cannot make it. Whatever you do, never let other people's opinions become your reality.

My year one teacher thought I was not good enough and I would probably not amount to anything, as did some of my high school teachers. However, once I decided I was going to go to university there was no stopping me; I was going to go to university and I was going to graduate, even when I had depression I still made it. I say to you that once you decide what you want to do, just go for it. A lot of people will try to put you off and sometimes it will feel like you are going the wrong way because everyone is going the opposite way to you. The chances are you are the only person dancing to the beat of your own drum. A lot of people always want to conform to what other people are doing. At sixteen a lot of people in school had a clear plan they wanted to follow, but when a lot of their friends decided to follow something else they also decided they will do the same. A few years later they discover that they are not really good at that thing and they have to find a new plan. We were all born to win and we can only win if we do that thing that we were born to do. I say, do not look at the things other people are really good at, focus on the things that you are really good at. Les Brown put this way: "Imagine you were on your deathbed and the ghost of your dreams are all on your bed saying we came to you and you never used us." Walking through a graveyard I thought to myself how many great musicians and authors have taken all their great talents with them. Use the talents that you have and you will certainly get the results you want.

I think the best way to be successful is to become self-dependant; too many people rely on other people to live a happy life. However, they do not realise that by doing this they are giving away the power to control their lives. If you want to do something in life, do not focus too much on what other people will do for you or how they do a particular job. A lot of people copy the way other people talk, walk, and do a particular job and they try to do the job the same way. No matter how much you try you will never be the best copycat. You must always look at how best you can do a particular job without thinking about how your colleague will do it. If you do this, you will not be using the power that the Lord has given you. You have to make your own judgement on situations without worrying what other people will make of your judgement. Too many people worry about what other people will think of their decisions. I say whatever you want to do, make up your mind and just go out and do it with all your heart with the aim to finish what you are going to start. Do not let others influence your decisions: it is your life, you must decide what you want and not how other people want it. No matter how farfetched the dream that you are holding inside you might seem to be, do not listen to what other people say but instead listen to that little voice in the innermost heart and answer its call to go and be what you want to be. The only way you can *Arise and Shine* is if you are really depending on yourself and not on other people. You see, if you are only doing what other people are doing, this just becomes an unconscious habit. What you want to do is to train your mind to think of ideas and not depend on other people's ideas. George Bernard Shaw once famously said: "I got successful by thinking twice a week, the trouble with a lot of people is that they do not think at all." The majority of people do not think at all because they just want to rely on other people. If you are not able to think on your own, you will never be able to *Arise and Shine*; you will stay where you are and you will not be what you want to be.

The other way that helped me stay in control of my life was having faith that things were going to work out. Before I made the decision to take control my life I was an emotional wreck; I was always expecting things to not work out. If you think nothing will work out, you will not do the best you can because you know you are going to fail. I was failing in school because I expected to fail and the effort I put in reflected the fact that I was preparing to fail. So many people go through life expecting the worst. I think that the world we live in today is so negative and we often expect bad things to happen to people. One day I heard a song and the words in that song really made me sad. The lyrics said that the worst you gave me was the best you ever gave me. That does not even make sense but it also tells us that some people expect the worst in life. They think that all the bad things that happen to them are supposed to happen. They never see the light at the end of the tunnel; they are spectators of their own life and they are continuing to stand on the side lines. A lot of people are watching other people win all the time, admiring them, congratulating them and then they go back into their own world wishing things could be different. We get in life what we expect. In order for you to have control of your life you have to expect to win at everything you do.

There are a lot of things that happen today that we do not have control of. However, what happens to us does not have a bearing of where we are going to end up in life. One thing that a lot of people do not understand is that we have a choice in everything that we do in life. You have to make decisions based on what we want in our life and go for it. If you want to make changes in your life, you have to make a choice to decide what you want in your life. What a lot of people do not realise is that what we focus on we will feel. You might be focusing on the fact that you lost a job so you are going to be broke; other people say the economy is bad and they lost their job so they are going to find something. These are the people who achieve massive success because they have made up their minds to focus on what they can do about the situation that they find themselves in.

You should always look at what you can do about this instead of feeling sorry for yourself. You must always ask yourself, 'what am I not doing with my job that I can change? Why is my relationship not passionate? What can I change to make me the way it was in the beginning and not look at what can I change about my other half?' There is always something you can do, and how you respond to every situation will determine where you end up in life. One of the things I have always looked at in the jobs that I have done is whether I gave my all in this job or was I just cutting corners? Every time you cut corners you will think that you are cheating other people but you are only cheating yourself and one day you will be found out. "Les Brown said you can either pay now or pay double later". The meaning you give to things is what matters, if we associate a lot of pleasure with working hard and doing what we were born to do we will do it. Ultimately the meaning we give to an experience will determine where we end up in life. I worked with people with cancer for a year and one patient stood out. She was having her treatment but she decided she did not want any more and she did not eat anything because she had made a choice not to fight. I knew this other patient who was more focussed on why he should continue living; he is alive today because he refused to give up on life and the people he loved. Two people with the same chances of survival, but one of them chose the way to death because she thought that was the easiest way. Whatever your story is, you were born to win and you will win but only if you think you can.

Everything we have done in our lives was a result of a decision we made one day. A lot of us wake up one day and are like: how did I end up here, why is my life this way? It's because of all the little decisions that we made: you can choose your life, you can make the right choice, and life is always asking every day for us to make those little changes. However, a lot of us do not make those changes. We continue living the life we want—or do not want in some cases—until one day life decides not to ask for these changes but demands them.

We borrowed a lot of money as a society. The banks were lending money to anyone and everyone, despite what their income was and life was calling for these changes and in 2008 it demanded them, everyone had to change. You have to make little changes in your life every day. You have to start watching less television. You have to spend more time with the people you love. You need to feed your mind with things that will make you grow. If you do not do this, one day you will find that you are not at the same level as the other employees in the organisation and life will demand change from you in the harshest possible way. Perhaps by your employer relieving you of your duties. You see, when a ship is sinking, the things that a lot of people do not find valuable will be thrown overboard to enable the most valuable cargo to survive. In whatever you do, you must make sure that you are making yourself valuable and creditable in the job that you are doing. I always say to people that you are not doing it for your boss, you are doing it for yourself. There might not be an opportunity for promotion in your job right not, but I bet someone is watching you, maybe one of the suppliers or one of the organisations your organisation works with. Ultimately what I am trying to say is that as long you make up your mind to work hard, no matter how bad things are, you are going to get your reward.

I have heard a lot of people say they have worked hard but they have achieved nothing in life. I believe this is because a lot of people have a lot of jobs but they are just wandering generalities. They go from one job to the next, they do the best they can do in it, but they do not like it very much so they move on to the next one and so on. I say to you that you must aim to become a meaningful specific; find what you love doing and do it as if your life depended on it. Do it while you have a lot of energy because our bodies change and very soon we might not be able to do these things. I believe that if we all made up our minds to do what we were born to do then the world would be very wealthy. A lot of people lack the burning desire to be the winner that they were born to be. Oh! to live a life only to discover that you never lived at all. Some people do not use life, they are just getting used up by life. Les Brown once said; "we should not leave this world with a full tank but we should leave with an empty tank." Even if it might not help somebody alive, it might help somebody years after you are gone. What am I trying to say? I am saying: make up your mind about what you want and simply go for it with all your strength and mind and you will achieve your goals. You have to do everything that you are required to do because there are no lifts to the top; you have to take the stairs every step of the way, one step at a time. And success might take years to come, but you have to keep going and never give up at all.

Everyone wants progress but they do not want to change. If you do a certain thing for long enough, it will become a part of you and the only way you can change is if you stop rewarding bad behaviour. I think society as a whole rewards bad behaviour in celebrities because people want to hear about that, and whatever they do some magazine will do an interview with them and give them a million pounds. Ask yourself what you are doing to reward your own failings and change it. I remember at one point in university I was reading Dr Ben Carson's book and I would go around saying to myself I can do what everyone can do but I can do it better. But I never changed what I was doing, so this did not make any difference to my life at all. The rewards for doing what you love and living the life you want are far more rewarding than the people who will take pity on you.

In conclusion to this chapter, you have to have control of your life and not let external factors affect where you end up in life. When you fail at something, the best way to overcome it is to start all over again and not spend time reliving your failures. You need to get started and you can only start where you are with what you have now. Remember, you do not have to be great to get started, you have to get started to be great. You must ensure that you become self-dependant. You must look to empower yourself and not just feed on other people because this is the only way you can use your talent. You must make sure you spend time with positive people who will empower you and not people who discourage you all the time. You must also make sure that you love people for who they are, because this is the only way you are going to get on with people. And remember, people are vital if you want to be successful. In whatever you do, you must expect the best all the time; you must always expect to win and if you do this you will *Arise and Shine!*

Chapter 7

Faith

I alluded in the previous chapter to the fact that we become what we expect. I really believe, from the bottom of my heart, that we become what we think we can become. There are very few people who have achieved all their goals in life because there are very few people who think they can achieve all their goals. People always want to do something they are comfortable with. Remember the example of choosing what university course to do; most people chose what they thought they would find easy without realising that if you really want to achieve highly in life, easy is not an option, you have to work really hard. If you think your life is not where you want it to be, you need to start doing things you are scared of. A lot people fail in life because they repeat the same things that made them fail in the first place and they expect different results. If you keep doing the same things you have been doing, you will continue getting the same results. I think the only way that you will ever become successful is if you have faith that you are going to become what you want to be and if you do what you need to do. The Bible in the book of Hebrews says: "Now faith is being sure of what

we hope for, being convinced of what we do not see."
We have to be really convinced that we are good enough
to actually *Arise and Shine*. We have to believe that we
are good enough to be and do the things we want to do.

If your life has been difficult, it is difficult to expect
the best in life. I remember asking myself why I was
born. The day I failed my exam I answered this question
and my answer went like this: I do not know what the
purpose is but I will work hard to find out what my
purpose is in life. I was in the dark; I could not see the
light at the end of the tunnel. However, there was one
thing I knew: I had to start crawling out of the dark and
it did not have to be the next day but I had to start that
very moment. That very second, I became the focussed
person I am today. A lot of people did not see my
progress but my life was changed. I was a kid with low
self-esteem who was not very good at anything, but I
was going to work on that. For your faith to grow you
have to forget what you have achieved at that point in
time; you have to forgive yourself and move on
completely. You should never replay your past in your
mind. Take one step at a time – just because you have
failed does not mean you will amount to nothing.

Successful people will tell you how much they have
failed in their lives but all they had was the belief that
they were going to win if they kept going. I heard Les
Brown say "no matter how hard it is and no matter how
hard it gets, I am going to make it". The journey is
going to be long and hard, and people without faith will
not reach the destination. They will spend all their time
doing jobs they do not like because they do not feel they
are good enough to do anything better in life. They will
not do anything that they want to do. They go to work,

they look after the family, and they die believing they are not good enough to do what they really want to do. I remember listening to Les Brown tell his life story. He talked about how he would struggle to speak in front of people when he started and how he thought he was not good enough. I listen to him now and he is one of the best motivational speakers in the world.

The Bible says that you shall know the truth and the truth shall set you free. The truth is that you do not have to be great to get started. The truth is that if you work very hard, you will achieve your goals in life. However, the lie that we have told for generations and generations that only very few people are chosen to indulge in the cake of life is false. The reality is that there is a slice for everyone in the cake of life; you just have to do what you need to do. Thomas Edison said, "People who fail in life are those who give up and what they do not realise is that they were really close". The truth is that every day you make that one step in the dark, you are getting closer to your goal. Every time I increased my marks by a percentage, I knew I was getting closer to what I wanted. When I started my A levels I always said that I may not be what I want to be but I sure thank the Lord I am not what I was. I knew I was becoming a new person day by day. I had a direction and I knew where I was going. A lot of people know where they are going, but they do not look beyond the obstacles. They focus on their limitations and they do not become what they should be. You can do more than you are doing only if you think you can or even if you want to.

I believe that I started growing when my faith started growing; the bigger my faith got, the more I believed that I could go to university and the more work I did. If you truly believe in what you are doing and what you can do, you will make it. A lot of people focus on what they are not capable of doing at that particular time, however, the thing that a lot of people do not realise is that you can learn all you need to know. Do not look at how other people are doing their work, you can make it on your own!

One thing that stopped me a lot of times was fear. Fear kills dreams, fear destroys relationships, and fear destroys lives. In chapter four I talked about the unknown heaven and how people are so afraid to venture in places they are not sure about. We all want to do things we feel comfortable with and to work with people that we know very well. However, if we were to settle for the things that we feel comfortable with, we would not achieve anything in life, we would live mediocre lives. You have to step out of your fears and step into your greatness, which a lot of people do not do. They remain in fear all their lives. I think the best way one can overcome fear is to do the things that we are afraid of doing. The little things that we are afraid of are the things that will determine whether we are going to *Arise and Shine* or we are going to fail in life. The best way to approach life is to fill yourself with faith; you have to see yourself as a normal human being. You have to feel you are really human and you can do everything other people can do and there is one thing that you can do better than anyone. If you fail now and again, you might believe that you are not capable of living a successful life. William James said that: "the greatest discovery of my generation is that man can change his life by changing his attitude of mind." You can change your life by putting more positive things into your mind and not focusing on your weaknesses.

The 23rd August 2007 created a new person in me because, for the first time, I was not focusing on my failures but I was more focussed on the possibility that was in front of me. Here I was in one of the richest lands in the world and I was a high school failure. However, all I could see round me was possibility after possibility. I then realised that we all live in a land full of opportunities. George Bernard Shaw once said that "the people who get on in life are the people who look for opportunities and if they can't find them", they create them. The people who create the opportunities that they want have a deep rooted faith that tells them whatever they are going to do is going to work out. When my friend Libby went into business by herself, she truly believed that she was going to make it. She did not have much capital, but what she had was a plan and a brain to produce what she wanted.

To be successful in life a lot of people focus on the resources that they actually have rather than the resources they do not have. Some people are successful in life because they know the right people or they know somebody who knows the right people. When I started on this journey of personal development, I did not know anyone who was in personal development, all I knew was that if I kept knocking, a door would be opened. One day after Sunday morning service, I went to two churches to see if I could speak to their youth about my journey. In the first church I visited, I was quickly told this was not possible; I said my polite thank you and I moved on to the next church. I got in just as service was finishing and once the service had finished, I rushed to talk to their minister who spoke to me and invited me to come and speak to the congregation. I had never spoken to a live audience before; I always speak in my church but this was the first time I had spoken to strangers. The people who make it in life are those who look for circumstances that they want in life, and if they do not exist, they create them. I could see the opportunities to speak so I went in search of them.

The Bible says: "Seek and you shall find, knock and the door will be opened." You have to go in search of what you want in life – this is the only way your dreams are going to be realised. You have to do it in the knowledge that if you seek, you will surely find your heart's desire. I was speaking to this young black man on the train and he looked at me and said: "It's really sad to be black isn't it mate?" Knowing what he meant, I asked him to reiterate and he said, "Because we are black we can never achieve anything because there will always be people to tell us we are not good enough." I said I have faith that if I do what I am supposed to do and work hard, I will achieve my dreams. Faith looks at big things in the world, fear looks at the reason you might not achieve your goal. Faith is the only weapon you can take with you in the fight called life; if you have faith, you will win, and if you take fear, you are certainly going to be defeated like the majority of people. The fight called life is only won by people who believe they deserve the best that life has to offer and they equip themselves with inspirational things and look for opportunities to become what they want to be. You see, while other people are following other people's trails other people are looking to create trails for other people to follow.

In order for you to create your own trail you have to have total faith in yourself. You see a lot of people depend on other people to help them get what they want all the time. They do not do anything and make their own judgement whether the work they have done is adequate enough. I remember when I worked for a gentleman whose wife was my fiancée Suzie's friend. It was the two of us in the office and from the start the other person was telling my boss what I was not good at. I decided to ask my colleague to judge every bit of work that I was doing – well I let him anyway. My boss had asked him to check my work all the time and I thought I would just let him check every bit of the work that I was doing. I did not have faith in my own abilities so I was not progressing. It was not a very pleasant experience. I went to work not enjoying a single day and thinking I was not really good at my job. Well, I was not good at my job because I did not have faith in myself. I believe that if people believe they are good enough at something, they will just go right out and do it without waiting for anyone to tell them what they need to do. You see when you are depending on other people to tell you what to do you are just using their brain and not using your own brain.

A lot of people are not successful because they do not think at all; they just do things other people have thought about. I remember a lot of times in high school, the teacher would ask a question and I would just think it was wrong and some clever kid would answer the question and I would be like, huh, I was right. I never trusted my abilities, so much so that I always surprised myself when I answered a question correctly. Working in hospital has exposed me to working with a lot of people in higher places like consultants which has made me realise something about people. In reality, most people are not as confident as they seem to be. They may walk and talk confidently all day long but when they go home, when no one is looking, there are tears or worries about something they have done. Most of the time we spend being afraid of people who are afraid of their shadows when no one is looking. Have faith in the fact that you have what it takes to be successful and do not look at what other people can do: think about what you can do very well and you can if you think you can.

The other thing to do when things get really hard is to have faith that things will work out somehow. When I was in my second year of university, I was suffering with depression and went to my exam just hoping for a miracle (which actually happened!). I was struggling in one of my modules, which I never really understood at all. In the exam, we had to choose two questions from four. We had six topics to revise and I knew I was not going to do it so I just revised two topics and just hoped that the two questions would be in the exam. The next day in the exam the two topics I chose came up. I have never been a fan of last minute revision, I always like giving myself time to learn everything properly, but I found myself having to do this. I did very well in the exam.

I could have given up and said that everything had fallen apart and what is the point of even going to the exam now. But something inside me said all was not lost, I could do something with what I have got left if I put the work in. A lot of people give up because they think it is too late to do anything about it, so they do not do anything to get the outcome that they want. No matter how hopeless things seem to be at the moment, just be hopeful that things will work out and you must ensure that you continue to do what you need to do. Two days before my exam all I knew was that I only had enough time to learn two topics properly so I learnt two topics very well. I did not look at how many topics I needed to learn, I just knew I needed two and expected a miracle. I did not just hope for one I expected one, therefore I made sure I learnt the two topics very well. I am a big Manchester United fan and watching them under Sir Alex Ferguson was a joy. They would be losing and thinking all was lost when they would come back and win the match. Listening to people like Gary Neville talking about what made them win all those matches was because they played till the final whistle. In life, it is not over until you win. If you do not give up, you will definitely make it in life. You have to keep working at what you are doing and when things are not going well just expect a miracle.

A lot of times people reflect on what they did wrong in the past. They always look at the time they failed at something and they believe that they are not good enough. Zig Ziglar described fear as "false evidence appearing real". We manage to convince ourselves that we are not good enough because of what we did in the past. I say you should look at the past as a way of learning, learn the lesson, and move on. Sometimes when you look at your past, you will see that there are some good things you did there. When I made a decision to go to university I was totally focussed on the positives that I had done in the past, which convinced me that it was possible to move on. Look at the good you have done and this will show you that you are a better-than-good person if you decide to do what you were born to do. You have to pick all the positive things in life and use them to build the person you want to be. When I graduated from university I looked at all the good things that I had done in primary school, high school and university and I found that I was good at more things than I thought. This is the only way you are going to discover what you are really good at. I think a lot of good attributes put together will tell you what your best attributes really are. This will give you an opportunity to see which of your best attributes are your strongest and this will tell you what you need to do to *Arise and Shine*.

You must have faith that you only failed because you did not use your best attributes and that if you were to do the same thing again, you would do better because you would use your strongest attributes. You must have faith that if you use these attributes, you will get what you want. I had a friend in whom I used to see glimpses of brilliance now and again, but he never really believed that he was good enough at all. This stopped him from doing really well in everything he was doing. He never looked at his brilliance but only looked at his shortcomings. This told him that he was not good enough even when he did a very good job at something; there he was this little voice in his head telling him that he was not good enough. I really believe that looking at your past in a positive way will change the way you think about yourself; if picking the bad points of your life destroys it, why not pick the good points and move forward and learn from the bad experiences and live a happy life?

The biggest mistake people make is comparing themselves with other people. They look at what other people do and not what they themselves do. When you start on the journey to becoming what you want to be, do not look at what other people are doing and how they are doing it. When you decide to start something, do not compare your results with people who have been doing it for years because if you do this, you will start convincing yourself that you are not good enough. The truth is that the other person has had experience to learn what they needed to learn; they have cried and fallen and because they never gave up they have achieved what they want.

You do not have to be great to get started, in fact you are never great when you get started. You do a lot of things wrong and all you need to do is learn from them and move on. All you have to do is start where you are with what you have, and do not worry about what you do not have, instead focus on what you have. A lot of people do not develop their abilities because they do not believe that they would be any good hence they end up setting their bars very low and they hit rock bottom. I have always thought the best way to improve your faith in your abilities is by doing things that you are really afraid of doing. As one of the books says feel the fear and do it anyway. This is the best way of increasing faith in your abilities, keep doing it and doing it until you become familiar with what you need to do.

People will always tell you they can't do something because they have not done it before. I remember when I was in high school I was known as the worst person when it came to graphs. I did not do very well in anything that had graphs in, so when I decided I was going to sort my life out I decided to work on graphs and by the end of three years I finally understood them. Tony Robbins once said that "practice does not make perfect but perfect practice make perfect". You must make sure that you spend a lot of time improving yourself. A lot of times we spend time with other people and when we are alone we do not know what to do with ourselves; we depend so much on other people and do not endeavour to improve our skills at all.

Have you noticed that you may do the best job and your boss will not call you in to thank you for the work and give you encouragement, however, as soon as you make a simple mistake you are in the boss's office? I found this out in working in the office whenever I put extra hours in to ensure that the work was done to a required standard, no one said a thing to me about the work that was done. I found this really demoralising because it felt like all my weaknesses were being picked on and my many strengths forgotten. A new lady joined our department and, to be honest, from the moment she joined she always spoke about retiring. She was nearly retirement age and she struggled in work as well. I questioned my managers decision to give her the job from the start. Six months later I was proven right because this woman just never picked up the work at all. Everything she did not do, I was answerable for, which was really frustrating. My team leader was her friend so I did not stand a chance. My opinions were not going to be taken seriously because the two were close friends. What do I do now I asked myself? Walking home, I saw a car with a caption that said things are going just the way they are supposed to be and this made think of my situation at work and I said to myself out loud when I got home things are going the way they are supposed to!

At that I point I realised that everything that had happened to me in the past happened just the way they were supposed to. I really think that if I had passed my high school exams, I would not have become the person that I am today. A lot of people fail at something in life and they decide to stand back and be spectators of the game called life. They miss out living the life that they want because they believe nothing will ever go right. I think having the attitude that says everything is going as it should be going shows you all the good points that have come back from your bad experience. There is a hymn I learnt when I was 14 years old and it says we will live as God has planned, though at times we may not understand. You might not see the light at the end of the tunnel but you must keep moving.

What if you have done all you needed to do, lost sleep over it, and put your health on the line for the job and you do not receive the recognition you deserve? A lot of people in this situation give up and stop working hard and they just do enough to not get fired. My manager called me into her office to have a meeting with her and my team leader. I knew what the meeting was going to be about. I was the best performer in my team, and here I was, sat in front of my team leader and my manager who were questioning my performance. I had worked so much the previous months that I had become ill. Here I was, sat in front of two people, whose support I wanted and they were not giving it to me. I think a lot of people in this situation would get very angry and wonder why they were doing what they were doing. I did not do that. Instead you must look at the big picture.

Here is what I realised after this meeting: you will do the best you can and some people will still want to question your work. The trap that a lot of people fall into is not doing their best work after their best work is questioned. I was the best performer in the team, so how can you put me on a performance review, unreal. On the other hand, I realised that I was on the journey and that I have to continue doing the best. My boss was going to start watching my work and I thought I really did not deserve that. I thought I should be sitting in the office with my boss telling me how well I was doing, but this was not the case. You have to have total faith in yourself and your abilities because other people will question them. I got out of the meeting with my head still held up high because I knew my work was up to the required standard. When people tell you that you are not good enough all you have to do is keep going because if you stop doing the work then you will be worse off. You have to keep going forward and do not look back or take notice of people who put you down. The first thing I said to myself was to be still and think properly about what I had been told. I had enough faith in my own abilities so much so that I did not react to what I was told but I acted on what I knew I could do. I knew people were going to be watching me; I knew people would always report back on what I do. However, I had so much faith in what I was doing, I had seen it work. One of the things that got to me was the fact that I was accused of not being patient-centred in my dealings, although I considered that to be the strongest attribute I possessed in my job.

I found that sometimes you have to just say things are going the way they are supposed to go. Sometimes you are going to work really hard and people will not recognise your work: work hard anyway, you will be honest and frank and people may not be happy with you but be frank anyway. People will forget the good you have done to them tomorrow, do good anyway. Remember everything that you are doing you are doing for yourself and not for other people. A lot of people say their boss doesn't like them so they will do minimal work. After the meeting with my boss I would have said that I will not work hard anymore, I will let the whole place fall to pieces so that I can show them that they needed me.

Listen, if your current employer doesn't value and won't even consider you for a promotion at all: do not worry. Do the best you have to offer and an opportunity will come up one day. A lot of people want everything yesterday, but it does not work like that. You have to move forward one step at a time and take each day as it comes. So many people either think about what happened to them in the past or what might happen in the future so they do not live in the present. In our heads, we create all these things and they become reality. When I was told I was not good enough in my job and I thought I was being blamed for what was going wrong in the institution I was working in, I would have taken this to heart and said I was not good enough or I would have said they were the ones who employed the wrong person now I am doing the job well. However, I decided I was going to continue doing what I thought was best for the patients and what would make me grow as a person. I refused to let this incident affect my performance; I was going to continue doing what I do best no matter what other people are going to put on me.

Why was I doing this when people did not seem to appreciate the time I gave up ensuring that the department was running smoothly and I did not get the reward I thought I should have? I thought people should have been singing my praises for the work that I was doing but they didn't; they just told me what I was doing wrong and blamed me for everything that went wrong. I spent a whole weekend wondering where I had gone wrong and this is what I found out: people will try and find someone to blame when things go wrong to cover their own backs. They will get around the problem, especially if it is their mistake, by finding a member of staff to blame.

I always tell people that no matter what they are going through, things will work out in the end. However, a lot of people do not look beyond their troubles therefore they end up living unhappy lives. Whatever you are going through at the moment has not come to stay, it has come to pass. People who go sailing will tell you that there might be rough waters on the journey, but they will pass and the sea will again be calm. You may just be wondering how you are going to get out of the trouble you are in, but I say just look at what is ahead of you if you keep going. A lot of people fail at something and they count themselves as failures; they remind themselves of their past failures and they sit down and watch their lives go by. They have the best ideas but just because they failed in the past, they class themselves as failures and they give up on their dreams and themselves. They end up doing jobs they do not like at all and miss out on living a happy life.

Do not let other people decide where you are going to end up in life: if you want to do something, just go and do it. Do not worry about what other people think: just do what you want to do. Can you imagine if you

156

were on your deathbed only to realise that you did not do anything you were born to do just because you thought it would not work out or you thought you were not good enough? A lot of people go through life thinking this way and they do not achieve anything. They live their lives with regrets and they leave this world wondering what they might have achieved. You are here now and instead of wondering what could be, go and make it a reality. After my exam results I wondered what to do, but do not forget the lesson you have learnt from that experience. From failing my exam, I learnt that if I put in the work and effort, I would get the results that I wanted. A lot of people when they fail do not look at how it could be if they worked hard from that day and rather than what could have been. Try something and it does not work out, learn the lesson and move on completely to your next challenge. You must have faith that if you do the work, you will do better than you did last time. We can all do better than good; it is just a few people who are willing to work better than just hard enough. I think that is why Zig Ziglar said that there are no traffic jams on the extra mile: very few people are willing to go that extra mile because they do not have a lot of faith in themselves.

The other thing that I think is making a lot of people unsuccessful is the lack of faith in other people. I had very little faith in my colleagues, so much so that I thought that I had to do it all. When you do not have trust in other people, you do not help them to get what they want and, in the end, I did not get what I wanted. You see, having faith in people helps you have people around you who will help you. Having faith does not mean having faith just in oneself, but also in other people. There are a lot of things going on today and a lot of people do not trust each other. Globalisation has made it easy to connect with the world in a short space of time, but human beings do not trust each other at all. People are divided by skin colour, religion, nationality and class. We only trust the people we are close to, or we have known for a while.

Next year I am getting married to the love of my life who is white, but to me I am engaged to a woman and that's all. We'll probably be put in a box of a mixed-race marriage, but for me we are two people who are in love with each other. Every race of people has put a label on another race and this has stopped a lot of people interacting with each other. This lack of trust has made the world miss out on a lot of things. I think that this world would have been a better place if the whole world just got on. We associate certain groups of people with certain crimes and this has made a lot of people lose faith in other people. What we have forgotten in all of this is that criminals are criminals and that is all. In every race and religion you will have the good, the bad and evil. A lot of people with great talents have not been given a certain job because of the labels that people have put on a certain group. I am not saying you do not have to be vigilant about who you trust, but a lot of people do not give other people a chance to prove themselves.

I believe that if people had more faith in each other, things would be achieved in the world. Every group of people wants to be trusted but they do not realise that they will only achieve this if they trust other people. I believe that human beings are generally good, despite what is going on in the world today. If you go looking for the bad in people, believe me you will find it, and if you go looking for the good, you will find that too. However, a lot of people go looking for the bad and they find it and this has created so much tension among people. People will help you to get where you want to be, so if you do not trust people you will not learn from them. Believe that learning from other people is the best way that you can learn. Have faith in people; do not be afraid to trust, but at the same time, use your brain to make the right the judgement and do not just act on what other people say.

In conclusion, to be successful in life you have to have faith that things will work out as they are supposed to in the end. No matter how bad things may be or will get, you must just tell yourself that you are going to make it because things are going just the way they are supposed to. A lot of people expect that things will not work out and, in the end, they do not work out. You should always expect the best no matter how bad things are going. If you expect the worst, you will always get the worst because we become what we think about. If we have faith in ourselves, we will achieve what we want to achieve if we think we can.

Go for what you want with all your heart and never listen to what other people are telling you. Just do what you think is right. I have always said to people: do what you can do and the Lord will do what you cannot do. In other words, do what you can and other things like opportunities and knowing the right people will take care of themselves. Things will be sorted once you know what you need to know. You do not have to be great to get started, you have to get started to be great; you must have faith in other people and really believe that people will help you in your life. Help other people get what they want and you will get what you want. If we want a better world, we must have faith in ourselves, our abilities, and we must also have faith in other people, if you do this you will *Arise and Shine!*

Chapter 8

Plan, Prepare, Expect

I believe that there are three steps in life that will determine whether you are successful or not. I first came across these steps after listening to the great Zig Ziglar talking about how to become successful. I believe that a lot of people are not successful because they have not taken these three steps. Too many people are going through life without a clear direction of where they want to go; they believe that things will just work out somehow. Things in life do not just fall into place without us taking consistent and constructive action. If you want to achieve something in life, you have to go for it with all your heart and do it as if your life depended on it, you know why? Because it does. In this chapter, I am going to give you the three steps that you must follow in order to *Arise and Shine*. You have to plan, prepare and expect to *Arise and Shine* in whatever you are doing. A lot of people do not succeed in life because they do not follow these steps, instead they go through life just existing.

The first thing that you must do if you really want to be successful is that you must have a plan of what you want in life. Listening to a few young people who were applying to go to university the other day got me really worried about young people today. Two of these bright young people were talking about applying to university and it soon become clear that they did not have any idea of what they wanted to do after university or what opportunities their courses would bring. I feel that schools are more concerned about league tables and how many people they are going to get into universities, neglecting to teach people about truly planning their futures. The best advice I would give to a young person like that was take a year out and really think what you want to do in life.

George Bernard Shaw once said: "I got successful by thinking twice a week, the trouble with a lot of people is that they do not think at all." And I think the school system has neglected one of the biggest aspects of life which is thinking. A lot of young people are not encouraged to think outside of the box and focus on what they are really good at. This is reflected in so many ways. For example, if a student is not very good at maths but really good in geography, teachers will harp on about how they are not good in maths, so much so that they lose confidence in themselves and they become bad at geography too. I believe that the school system should include time for thinking to encourage young people to think and plan their future. For a lot of young people, a lot of things seem to just surprise them. It's like they are walking alone. Before they know it, they find themselves with a wife and then more mouths to feed, rent to pay, and they do not know what to do next. The truth is that these are all events we can plan for. They can happen to everyone in life, so the chances are they will happen to you at some point. It shouldn't be a big surprise, it has to be something you have planned for.

When Suzie and I are going to visit someone for the first time, the first thing we do is check how far away the place is and how long it is going to take us to get there, and also find a place to stop on the way for refreshments. We work out how much petrol we will need to get there and back. The journey is all worked out and planned. One of the things we make sure of is that we check if there is an accident on the motorway what our alternative route is. We work out how we are going to get there and work out alternative routes just in case of unexpected events on the road. I believe that a lot other people do this when they are embarking on a long journey. Well, life is a long journey with a lot of unexpected events on the road, but why do a lot of people just let it take them for a ride instead of staying in control?

Many people work every day without knowing what they want to achieve that day, that week, or that month. You have to live each day of your life. Life is a gift from God and what we do with life is the gift we give back to God. I suggest that if you have not done this that you write down a plan of where you want to go in life and also work out what alternative routes you can take, just in case the path is blocked. It is important to know your destination but also to work out different ways you can get there. A lot of people are not successful in life just because they only know one way to get where they want to be. For example, young people going to university work their socks off and expect that they will have a very good job straight out of university. They finish university and these opportunities are nowhere to be seen at all, what do they do? They might say they have worked so hard and still have no fruits for their labours. A lot of people will give up from here, not realising that they are close to their goal. Here is what I did once I left university: I found unpaid work in charity shops and other charitable organisations to give me the experience I needed to compete with other people who already had experience in what was a very difficult market. I did not go straight into a job after leaving university. I knew that the job search might be hard but I had a goal and a dream to find work so I set a second plan to help get employment when I left university. You see the people who get on in life are the people who look for opportunities that they want in life and if they do not find them, they create them.

The sad fact is that we have hundreds of thousands of people in British universities today, probably the highest proportion of young people in university ever, but a lot of them will come out without a clear plan of what they want to do with their lives. A lot of them live at home with only one plan to get out of their parents' home and enjoy the freedom that comes with it. They do not think of what will come after that. They get to university, party a lot, and, before they know it, the three years have gone, they have a below average degree, and they have to compete for jobs with people who have spent three years planning their future and doing work experience to improve their chances of getting employment. They go back home after three years and have to go back to their parents' house and the false feeling of having freedom is gone again. They then have to look for work at the supermarket – what a complete waste of time! I'm not trying to denigrate supermarket employees, but if you went to university for three years and you come out of university with £36,000 worth of debt and you are working in a supermarket, maybe you should have just found a job in the supermarket in the first place; that would have saved you and your parents a lot of money.

You see, if you decide not to make a plan for life, life will make a plan for you and I promise you this: it will not be what you want. If you want to stay in control of your life, you have to plan what you want to do in life. You have to have a clear and definitive goal you are working towards. You have to know where you are and what you are going to do and what you want in life. I currently work with people who are older than me and, for some, it seemed that life has gone by in the twinkling of an eye. They say things like: "I sometimes think, what has happened to life, as it feels like it was just a couple of days. I sit there and think, no it was not two days it is really thirty years." You lived each day without a plan because you did not know where you were going. If we are going to be successful in life we have to have a clear plan of where we are going and how to use the opportunities that we have in front of us.

In order to do this effectively, we have to make time to plan our future. There was once a time when the only entertainment you could get was a few television shows and then the rest of the time would be spent reading a book or something else. Those days are long gone with the arrival of cable television where you can catch something at any time of the day or night. Then we have social media, which keeps people up all the time. They come home from work and they are talking with people who they were in work with all day long. They then sit down in front of the television, watch television till midnight, then they are too tired to do anything. They then go to bed without thinking about what they have achieved that day and what they need to do better the next day. I believe that so many people are not successful in life because of the box culture; they are either on the computer chatting with people or in front of the television. They do not realise that this affects their ability to plan their lives all together. Remember: we become what we think about, so I suggest that every time you come in from work, university, or school, you spend thirty minutes every day writing down what you want from your life or what you want to achieve from your job the following day.

You can never grow if you do not have plan. You have to have a plan and decide how much you want to grow in your life or how much you want to grow in your job by the end of the week. This will then give you a plan of action you must take to achieve your goals. When I decided I was going to go university, I wrote down a clear plan of what I was going to do in order to take me from being a high school failure to a university student. I clearly marked the areas I needed to work on even though I did not know how I was going to do this at that stage but I recognised then I needed to have plan for the future.

Here is what a plan does for you: it tells you where you need to improve and how you can improve on it. If you have not got a plan, you will not be able to tell where you are in your life at all, because you will not have anything to measure it against. Whereas if you have a plan, you will always see how much progress you are making in your life because you will have a measurable plan which tells you whether you are becoming a success or if you are failing. This will enable you to work hard to change the course of your life. People who have not got a plan will not know whether they are failing in life or not because they have nothing to measure it against. They have no planned targets to aim at and they just go through life just existing, not knowing where they are going and more importantly what they want to do in life. You will only stay in control of your life if you actively decide you are going to participate in planning your own life, not leaving everything to nature to decide because you might not like it. You will end up helping other people achieve their own goals and dreams in life. Make use of the time you have now because the day will come when you will wish you had spent a little bit more time planning your own life.

However, having a plan is not enough to make yourself successful. I remember when I was living in Zambia I used to see people preparing for their high school exams. They would devise a well written study timetable which clearly had what they were going to study on a particular day, well labelled and clearly stated. However, on many occasions I would see these people sat outside talking and playing with their mates at the time when their timetable said they had to be studying. What was going on here? These people had a clear and defined plan that they were working towards. However, they made their plan worthless because there was no action involved in these plans. In order for you to be successful in life you have to prepare to be successful and the only way you can do this is by putting your well thought out plans into action. A lot of people are not successful in life because they do not put their plans into action. Whilst writing this, I am listening to a conversation outside my window and I have just become intrigued because there is a man outside telling his friends how he is going to start his own business and his friends have just said, you have been saying that for twenty-five years.

I was dying to get involved in this conversation. I went and took some rubbish to the bin so I could listen to this conversation properly. This man has a plan; he knows how much he needs to sell in the first year to break even. I am stood their thinking well you know what you need to do and with a plan like that you can be successful in a short space of time. His friend then asked him if he will get started soon. He replied with: "Maybe I might, I'll need to just think about it a lot more."

I'm thinking your plan is well detailed, you do not need to think it through you just need to get started mate! This is a lot of people's biggest problem: they don't get started at all, and they take all their greatness to the grave with them. The two men then went their separate ways and I thought to myself: I bet if I met you in five years' time, he would still have that plan in his head and would still have done nothing about it. That is the story with a lot of people, they all have the best laid plans, but they do not amount to anything because they do not take action towards their plan. The people who make it in life are the people who take action all the time. If you take action with your best laid and defined plans, you will get the results that you want in life; if you do not, they will just be plans on a piece of paper, which does not mean anything to anyone.

The first thing to do is look at your plans as the things you need to do in order to be successful in life, which is all plans are. You have to spend time looking at your plan and then prepare to be successful by working out what you need to do and then going out there and doing it. The man outside my window knew exactly what he needed to do, but he was not doing it, hence twenty-five years later he was having this conversation with his old friend outside my window instead of running three or four stores of his own. If you have a plan and you know what you need to do, fine. If you are not certain, just go right out and do it anyway, feel the fear and do it anyway! Your plan is telling you what you have to do to be successful but for a lot of people they look at their plans and find a reason why they are going to fail or why it will never work out for them. If it worked out for other people, it can also work out for you. All you have to do is keep working on your dreams and your best laid plans.

One of the things that stops people from living their dreams and going through with their plans is the fear that they are not good enough. A lot of people feel that they are not good enough to achieve their dreams, but I believe that the best action you can take is to feed your mind with positive things. As Zig Ziglar said: "we are all where we are and what we are because of what goes into our minds and we can change where and what we are by changing what goes into our minds."

We listen to a lot of things these days and most of it is negative. Have you ever notice how most of the time people are told negative things? A child goes to school and the parents say: "Be careful and make sure you do not get run over." It's either doom, or we are talking about how bad the weather is going to be the following day. The other day I heard a song and the lyrics of the song kind of confused me a little because they said, 'the worst you gave me was the best I ever got.' If we are filling our minds with negative things, our best laid plans will not become a reality because we will find a reason why we are not good at something. I believe that a lot of people would have put their plans into action had they not looked at the work other people have done. Listening to other people will not make you become what you want, neither does comparing yourself with other people. In order to put you plans into action and to prepare yourself to live your dreams, you have to do the things that you are afraid of doing. When you start something, you will not always get it right the first time but as Les Brown says: "Anything that is worth doing is worth doing badly."

Why? Because until you know how to do something better, you will continue doing it badly. Do not look at other people who have had years of experience working the things you want to do. Tell yourself this: you do not have to be great to get started, you have to get started to be great. The great people you look up to all the time had to get started somehow. They also had to experience failure and disappointment, and people telling them they are not good enough. A lot of people have made their plans but people have told them they are not good enough or their idea won't work and they have given up without ever trying to put into practice something they spent years planning.

If you find yourself going a different way from other people, do not be discouraged, just keep going. This is because you are dancing to the beat of your own drum.

A lot of people are dancing to the beat of other people's drums just because they have refused to dance to the beat of their own drums. What do I mean? I mean a lot of people are helping other people live their dreams; they have given up on their dreams and now they are employed by somebody who has put their plans into action even though people told them they were not good enough. They go through life wishing they could have done this, that, or the other, they wish they had not listened to this one or that one. You must stop waiting for other people to tell you what you are good at and just go and do it.

"Be ye not conformed to this world but be ye transformed by the renewing of your mind." Put the good, the positive and the pure in your mind, and listen to positive and uplifting materials. Remember that the worst experience in your life can be the best teacher, you just have to prepare for what you want by thinking positively all the time and on your dreams. The other thing you must do is love yourself for who you are. A lot of people are always saying they wish they were like this one or that one; love yourself for who you and not the other people wish you could be.

The best way one can prepare to be successful is by helping other people get what they want. We as a generation have become so individualist more than any other generation in history, everybody is always thinking about themselves and themselves alone. What a lot of people do not realises is that we have to help each other to achieve what we want. Other people will also help us get what we want. I think a lot of people have completely neglected this and they are more focussed on what they want in their own lives. I believe that if people looked at what they could give other people, they would then easily get what they want. Here is an example: you are working in a business and you want to be successful, you want to earn more money, what do a lot of people do in this situation? Complain that their boss is paying them very little. However, successful people think, how can I help my boss generate more profits? They put in more hours, they are the first in and the last out, and they do everything that they can do in their power to shape the future of the business. A person like this will soon receive the recognition that they rightly deserve. Two young people moved from Leeds in the north of England to Bristol in the west country hoping for a change in their fortunes in life. Three years later one of them was going back to his parents' house. Why? He said so he could find employment. On the other hand, the other young man was starting his own business and he was doing quite well. I think the difference between the two was one person was thinking what can this city give to me and the other person was thinking what do people of this beautiful city need.

There, ladies and gentlemen, you see the difference between people who are successful and who are not. People who fail in life are always thinking about what other people can do for them, while successful people are always thinking about what they can do for other people. If you are considering going into business, you must always think about what other people need and not what you need frompeople.

When I was doing my A levels I was working in a little convenience store and I noticed that fewer people were coming each and every day, why? I noticed that the owner of the shop was more focussed on making profits than making the customers happy. There were about four other shops that his customers could use. They did not feel that they were getting the best customer service so they decided to go somewhere else. He needed the people for him to be successful; we all need people to be successful ourselves.

A lot of people go through life thinking they will be successful by doing things on their own. You see we all have different experiences and by learning from other people we will be able to do things we might otherwise not be able to do on our own. If I had thought about what the customers needed first, they would have been really happy and they would have come to the business to spend their money. They would have got the service they wanted and he would have got the money he needed in order to make the profit he needed for his business to succeed. In other words, you need to help other people to succeed and you will succeed. I walked into our outpatients' department office in work and the people in the department were always arguing about something. It soon became clear to me that a lot of them only thought about themselves. I thought: if only each member of the team was thinking about the needs of others, the department would be successful.

I honestly believe that people fail in life because they set their bars too low and hit; they make plans and they look at them and they think that that will be too much for them and they stop. People fail in life because they set their bars to low and hit. No matter how big the challenge is going to be, just go right out and do what you need to do. A lot of people do not realise that they have not used up 95% of their ability. This is what happens when you make a plan and then people remind you how you failed in the past. I met a guy I had not seen since 2007 and he reminded me that I failed in high school; my response was, "have you not changed your calendar since 2007?"

Then he had a very awkward smile with an embarrassed look on his face. You might be looking at your plans at this point in time and thinking you have not achieved anything you set out to do in your life. This is not the time to throw away your plans, it's time you got started.

"Where do I start Frank?" Start where you are and with what you have, that's all you need – nothing else. You have all you need in yourself, all you need to do is to get started and everything will work out in life if you put your plans into action. I once heard John Maxwell say "I wish you could have met me when I was not as good as I am right now". I also wish a lot of us could have met people we look up to when they were not good, I think this would make us believe that we can do the same. You must really believe that you are good enough to do what you want in life and go for it. You know why people cannot see it for you? It was not given to them, it was given to you and only you can do that thing better than anyone else.

So, you have planned and you have prepared by taking action, what else is left? Expectation. You have to expect that what you are going to do is going to work and that you are going to achieve the results that you want. We become what we think about; if we expect to fail, we will fail and if we expect to succeed, we are going to succeed. You see it has nothing to do luck at all. If you want to truly *Arise and Shine*, you have to expect that whatever you are planning is going to work. Can you imagine looking at your best laid plan and something in your mind says that is not going to work? You know what is going to happen? It will not work. If you expect something to work, no matter how bad things are, you are going to continue working on your plans because you are expecting things to get better. I heard of a young man who wanted to start a business in the city of Gloucester but was discouraged because of the recession. Everyone told him how it was not going to work, how he was going to lose all his money. A few years later the economy picked up and now he wishes he had carried on with his plans. He never did what he wanted to do because he was expecting the worst all the time. People had told him that if he went ahead with his business, he would not make it at all and he listened to them. I asked him if he had a plan of how he was going to make the business work despite the economy and he said that he did. He had a clearly defined plan of how he was going to make his business work but he listened to other people and they lowered his expectations.

People fail in life because they set their bars too low and hit and not because they set the bars too high and miss. Your expectations determine how successful you are going to be in life. If you expect to be successful, you are going to aim high, and if you expect to fail in life, you are not going to aim at all. This is true for a lot of people, they go through just existing and do not aim at anything in life because they do not expect the best in life. Whereas people who expect the best in life are always aiming at something. They always have a goal to achieve in life every day. They have that sense of achieving and feeling of aiming for something when they wake up each day.

You must aim at something and expect to do very well in the things that you are doing. If you are doing something and you think and know that that thing will not bring you any success in life, it is time to stop. If you think something is going to work, you are going to have passion for doing it. If you put passion into everything that you are doing, you are going to open doors that a lot of people think will never open.

I remember one day talking to a person in work and I saw that they never had any life in them at all. I walked to the reception desk where they were sitting and I thought if I was the person going up to that desk, I would not feel inspired at all. I currently work in a cancer unit and I believe that if the person on reception is alive all the time, the patients will start feeling alive. I think a lot of people are not alive because they do not have a passion for anything in life. Passion is the key that determines if you are going to make it or not: if you are going to live a happy life, you must have passion within you, you have to have the desire to win. Zig Ziglar said "Desire is the mother of motivation desire". You have to be motivated to win and live a happy life. So many people go through life just existing and not amounting to anything. They go to work, they raise a family, and they die without doing anything they were born to do. Life is hard, there are no two ways about it. For you to do something very well, even in difficult circumstances, you have to have a passion for that thing. A lot of people are doing things they do not have a passion about, hence they are average and, in the end, they do not amount to anything in that job. They feel unhappy and unfulfilled in what they are doing because their true passion is burning inside of them and they know it.

To be truly happy in life you have to have a passion in what you are doing and know that you do not have to do something you do not want to do. A lot of people feel trapped in the jobs; they feel they will not be able to do anything else in life. However, a lot of them do not realise that they can get out; they are in a self-made prison they can get out of any time they want to. Instead they find every excuse to stay in this prison. When I decided I was going to go to university, I made school my passion. I was passionate about learning new things and spending hours studying the subject I wanted to study. It was my passion even though I was not good enough in the eyes of a lot of people; my passion showed everyone that I was good enough in the end.

I believe that to change your life you have to become a passionate person. You have to have power and desire burning in your eyes. I worked with a young mum called Charlene. I remember the day I met her I thought to myself: I'm going to like this girl. She had the desire to do well and I have never known anyone get things so well in a short space of time. And she was good! It was apparent to me very quickly that there was something about this young lady. She had a passion for something and I quickly found out what that was: giving her daughter the best life possible. When new people start in my department I usually spend a few days watching them to see if they are getting things right, but I did not have to do this with Charlene. Within a week of her being in the department, I was able to get on with what I was doing and she got on with what she was doing. At the same time, we had an older woman in our department who was near retirement. She was getting everything wrong, and you could tell her things until you are blue in the face but she still never got it.

Charlene wanted a good life for herself and she wanted to enjoy life whereas the older lady was always thinking about retiring. I think if somebody offered her money to retire tomorrow, she would bite their hand off. You have to have passion for everything you are doing. You are going to spend most of your adult life going to work. If you are doing something you are not passionate about that means you will most of your adult life be going to a job you do not like at all. This means you go to work with emptiness in your heart and you go home the same way. My passion to help others is the reason I am in my job, I go home feeling I have given hope to a patient who was giving up to keep going, or I have made a family that has not smiled in a long time smile again. This is my passion and my drive in the morning.

Do you know people who are not passionate about their job Frank? They do not say anything nice about their jobs and they do not spend time thinking about how they can better themselves at all. They do things the same way each and every day, and if you were to meet them three years later, their work ethic would still be the same, and the same ten years later. They would still be in the same position in the organisation and they would still be complaining about the same things.

You have to really decide what you are you passionate about. I heard a story about a man who had a good position in his organisation and after he retired he died within a short space of time. He never had time to enjoy the fruits of his labours because all he did was work and work. A lot of people think that being a workaholic is a very good thing and that it is the only way you will ever be successful. I can tell you, I would still be sitting at the desk at 8pm in the evening having started at 7:30am in the morning. Before long, I was ill and stressed out and I was constantly tired. I wanted to do very well in the job I was doing, but what I did not realise was that I did not have to do other people's jobs very well, I only had to do my own job very well.

Remember that passion is doing something that you really want to do. I was at a funeral of someone I knew very well and as we were there something struck me straight away: everyone was talking about the things that the person loved the most and was most passionate about. He was a good singer and guitar player. I straight away thought to myself, you can earn a living doing that, and, moreover, you will be doing something you are really passionate about when you go out to perform. A lot of us do everything in life except that one thing we are passionate about; we find every excuse in the world why we cannot do it. We were not created just to go to work, raise a family, and then die. We were created to do a lot more than that: we were born to win. We will win if we do that one thing we are passionate about.

My friend Anselm wanted to travel. We graduated from our respective universities and I went in search for a graduate job, which I never got by the way, but Anselm went for his true passion and that was to go travelling to Australia. What I liked about what he did was that he did not do what his whole family expected of him, he did what he was passionate about. He has loved it so much that he has not come back home yet;

he has even extended his stay down under. I think it could have been easy for Anselm to say he would just go to find himself a job like everyone, and I think he would have easily found one. Moreover, his father was an influential person in his organisation, but that was not his passion, his passion was to go travelling. We do not have to think the rest of the world is not doing it; if you feel strongly about something, go do that thing and never listen to what other people say to you. You must have a plan and then take constructive and consistent action. You must expect to succeed live your dreams.

To conclude this chapter I would just like to remind you of the three main steps that you must follow. Firstly, you must have a plan of where you want to go in life. This means you have to make time to make your plans and decide where you are going. The truth is that if you do not have a plan for your life, you are not going anywhere because you have not got anything to aim for in life. You have to make time in this busy world to think about your life and the direction you are going in and decide if it is the direction you want to go in. However, if you do not put your plans into action, they will be worthless because they will not give you the results you desire. To get the results you want you have to make sure that you do what you have written on your piece of paper. Once you put into practice what you have written down, you will start getting the results you want. You must ensure that you keep doing what you need to do in order for you to live the life that you want.

Acting on your plans once in blue moon will not make you successful; you have to take actions towards your goal every single day. So secondly, you must prepare to follow your plan. A lot of people are not successful because they have good intentions, but they do not take action towards those intentions. Good intentions without action will make you stay where you are right now; you will never grow at all and you will remain afraid of the things that you are scared of.

Last but not least, you have to expect to succeed in everything that you are doing. If you do not expect to succeed, the chances are that you will not put the best into what you are doing. In order to expect to win we have to have passion in what we are doing, we must have a burning desire to win in life. Once you have a plan, you will know what you need to do in order for you to succeed. Once you start doing what you need to do in order to succeed, no matter how bad things are, you will expect to win. Once you start expecting to win, the passion in what you are doing will grow. Expectation will drive you on each and every day. Expectation will make you stay up late and wake up early. Expectation will make you enjoy the journey. You will not dread waking up every morning and wondering if things are going to work out. Instead, you will wake up with joy and great anticipation of things to come and then you will *Arise and Shine!*

Chapter 9

Finish What You Start

The start of a new year has always been the most interesting time of the year for me for so many reasons. One thing that intrigues me a lot is when it comes to making new year's resolutions. For some people, they probably had too much turkey and Christmas cake during the holiday season and it is time to shed some pounds. Some people decide that they will change their lives for the better; they will do something that they have been meaning to do for years. One day on my way to the train station I saw a group of women jogging; the next day I only saw three instead of four. Before long I only saw one person jogging. I have to say, I still see her jogging away today.

You see a lot of people have good intentions but they do not see them through. They plan to do something but they stop once it gets too hard. I think that's what happened to the other three women: they just could not bring themselves to wake up every morning and go running again. The chances are that they have been doing this for years; they start with good intentions and a few days later they give up because it is not fun anymore. It is not as easy as they thought it was going to be. You must always remember that easy is not optional, you have to keep working at everything because it always works if you work at it.

The day I decided to go to university, I did not know very much about my subject of choice at all. I decided I was going to do a business degree because it was one of my stronger subjects and that was all I had. I did not have a lot of teachers who trusted in me or friends who were going to be there to support me in that year. All I had was people who were telling me I couldn't do what I wanted to do in life. I had people reminding me that I had failed, I never heard the last of it in my household. I was always reminded about the fact that I had failed. If people are always reminding you that you are a failure, it makes what you want to do even harder. I always thought to myself: if I think that life is hard now, how much harder would life be if I grow up and I cannot pay the rent? How much harder can life be if I am going to a job I did not like at all? If you do not give up on your dreams, you will one day find the things that bring you satisfaction; you have to keep going, no matter how long the journey is going to be. Look at it as having a key in your hand and trying a lot of doors and eventually one will open, hopefully the right one. However, it is important that we understand that you might not find the right door straight away. For some people it takes years, and for others decades, but they become successful in the end.

A lot of people endure to the end because they enjoy the journey; they see each day as being one day closer to their dream. Do not look at how you are going to get there; you must always look at how you can use each day to get closer to your dream. A lot of people do not make it to their dreams because they are always worrying about how they are going to get there. We are living in a fast-changing world and something that you are worrying about today might not even be relevant to you in the next five years. So why do you want to give up on your dream based on things that might not even happen? A lot of people have been so close to their dreams and they have just given up when they were days away from achieving them just because they could not hold on for a few weeks. Here is the truth that a lot of people choose to ignore: if you give up on the things that you were born to do, you are not going to be happy and if you are not happy, what else is there?

My mum together with my uncle and one of my cousins were going to a little village in the western part of Zambia. It was during the rainy season and this part of the country is very wet and usually floods. They got to a certain point and water was deeper than they thought, so all the men who were in the car had to get out and help push the van out of the water so they could continue on their journey. After fifteen minutes of pushing the van out of the waters they were able to carry on with their journey and get to their destination safely.

Can you imagine if they all just said this is too hard, let's just stay here and we'll get there somehow. They would not have got anywhere at all. If you decide that life has got too hard and that you are going to stop now, you are not going to get anywhere. Working with other people has given me great insight to why only a few people live their dreams. I think that's why Zig Ziglar said: "there are no traffic jams on the extra mile." This is because very few people are willing to move forward when things get difficult. What a lot of people do not realise is that there are no short cuts in life. No one will let you take a lift on the way up, you have to take the stairs. You have to walk up step by step and there is no other way you can go. A lot of people have tried to find short cuts to life and they have not managed to.

Some people have turned to crime and they have been arrested the very first day. Some people are successful in crime for a little while but the law always catches up with them and they end up with nothing. No matter how bad things may be at the moment, you have to keep going. You have to keep that plan with you every single day to remind you where you are going. When things get really difficult, you will have that goal to help you. It will give you hope and encouragement and also give you reassurance that things might not be going very well right now, but you will make it eventually. You must have complete faith in your plan and in your abilities to execute your plans. On your journey to what you want to be, you will discover that there are a lot of things that you do not know. You can, however, learn all this; you do not have to be great to get started, you have to get started to be great! A lot of people will tell you that they cannot do something because they feel that they are just not good enough compared to certain people they know. I heard John Maxwell the American author, speaker and pastor say: "I wish people could have seen me before I becme a great speaker." Do not be discouraged because other people are greater than you, you will be just as good as them, if not better, if you continue working on your dreams. If you stop, you will certainly not become great by accident.

Greatness does not happen by accident, greatness happens through hard work and you must not stop giving your best all the time. I came across a story on social media about three nursing home employees who refused to stop caring for the elderly patients even after management had moved away. They helped wash and cook for the people in the home. A lot of people give up on their dreams and their principles just because they have no money. Everything requires money in today's world but what a lot of people do not realise is that they have to take action before they should start thinking about money.

A lot of people look at how much money they have and they decide that they have not got enough to do what they want to do and they give up on their dreams. People who make it in life are not people with resources; people who make it in life are resourceful. If you want to be successful in what you are doing, you must stop looking at what you do not have and look at what you have. Remember I said earlier that you have to help other people get what they want and you will get what you want. You have to ask yourself what service you can give other people in order for them to give you what you want. You must use the power of your great mind to explore options you can use in order for you to achieve what you want to achieve. A lot of people will tell you how they are going to do that and focus on the 'how.' I think that this is not the right place to focus all your energy. I focussed on going to university because I believed that this was going to give me an opportunity to do what I wanted to do in life. I am saying to you today to focus on why you need to do something. If you focus all your energy on why you need to do something, you will not ask a lot of questions, you will just be resourceful and you will reach your goal. Why? Well, once you know why you are doing something, you will not worry about your bank balance or who is telling you it cannot be done; you will just go out and do what you need to do. Do not become a *how* person, become a *why* person because this is the only way you will get motivation to do what you need to do in order to be successful.

Sometimes when you think it is all done, it is not. I remember the first job I had when I graduated from university. I worked really hard and I was thinking I was working myself into a permanent contract; this was it for me I had finally found what I was looking for. Life had other plans though, this was not it and I was there for three weeks and I was let go. Sometimes we will look for something, for example a job or a new relationship, and then we find one and we think we have finally found what we were looking for and then it ends in a very short space of time. What do a lot of people do when they find themselves in this situation? They discard their life plan all together. They throw away all their plans and, in the end, they do not amount to anything. The first thing I did when I was told that the organisation I was working for had to let me go was to start looking for a new job straight away. I was disappointed but I knew that I had worked so hard to be where I was at that point and I was not going to throw it all away now. I still believed with all my heart that I was going to make it. I knew I had worked through very hard situations growing up and I was well-equipped to deal with what was going to come in the future. For a lot of people this would have been the end;

they would not have become anything in life despite the education they have obtained. I think the biggest lesson that we should all learn is that sometimes things will just not work, no matter how much effort we put in. We might have a boss who might not like us, or our colleagues might not like us because of how we speak or how we dress as I have discovered in my current employment. People will not like us because we are willing to stand for what we believe in while the majority of people are not. This is because everyone wants to please everyone else. I say to you, keep going and do not give up your beliefs and your dream. It is yours: protect it no matter what people say about your dreams, go out there do it anyway. People will tell you it has never been done before or you need a lot of money to do that. Well, if you decide you have not got the resources to do it, you will never achieve it anyway. The journey might be long but it will not get shorter if you do not decide to start today.

In 2004 and 2005 I was in boarding school in a rural area of the north-western part of Zambia on the outskirts of small town called Solwezi. I was very much involved with anything to do with my church choir as far back as I can remember, and, going to a smaller congregation, I was soon conducting the choir. One day one of the priests by the name of Setty Maseka, who also happened to be my maths teacher, and I were asked if we could go to a little congregation, which was deep down in the rural area. Vehicles barely went there but we had to get there somehow. It was going to take three and a half hours to walk there and then conduct the choir for an hour or two and then make the whole journey back. I remember the morning we had to go there I asked him if we really had to go all that far and he said: "the Lord will provide Mr Frank."

We started off and after thirty minutes walking we got to the junction where our local congregation was situated and I looked down the road and was thinking that it was going to be a very long journey. Then, all of sudden, I saw people who went to the same congregation as me when I was in my home town and they were driving past the congregation where we were going and gave us a lift. We got there a lot earlier than we expected and we found that the congregation had been gathered since morning because they had not had practice for a while and they were all waiting in anticipation. We had choir practice and we finished earlier than we thought we were going to finish so it was time to walk back. We walked to the road and I was looking where we were going and thinking again that this was going to be a long journey. It was at this point that we saw the mini bus that belonged to one of the teachers in our school in front of us and we jumped in it and we were home earlier than we thought we were going to be.

Why am I telling this story? The truth is that a lot of us are constantly worried about what is going to happen in the future to the extent that we do not get started; we do not do the things that we really want to do. I wanted to go with my priest but I was more worried about how I was going to get there and back. A lot of people do not do what they want because they feel that they do not know the right people. When I decided I was going to be a motivational speaker, I did not have a lot of connections; all I did was ask people if I could come and speak to the youth in their churches. I did not have resources but I was resourceful. I always thought I had something they needed and they had something I needed. They had young people they wanted to be motivated, and I needed experience to become a motivational speaker. I have heard a lot of older people say, "I wonder how that could have worked out if you did not stop?" I say ask yourself this, how will what I am doing now end up if I stopped doing it? How will life be in the next thirty years if I don't see this through until the end? Ladies and gentlemen, so many people are very short sighted. They do not see how things are going to be in the long term; they see things the way they are now and they think they're going to be the same forever and they throw in the towel.

Whatever you might be going through now has not come to stay, it has come to pass! The problem with a lot of people is that they give up on life when they can't see what they need to do to be successful. Sometimes when you want to be in the sun, you have to move with the sun. For example, if your company moves location and you still want to work with the organisation, you have to move with the organisation, and if you do not move with them, they will have to let you go.

The world is changing so fast day-by-day and if you really want to live your dreams, you have to change with the world. You have to embrace change. You have to accept that change is good, even though the majority of people you meet will tell you that that they do not like change at all. However, it is needed to make organisations successful and empower employees. So, imagine you have been working on a dream in a certain industry and suddenly it all changes and you find that you do not do as much as you used to before things changed. I know a man who had worked in a certain industry for years and that was all he knew – or so he thought. He left the job he had done for fifteen years because things had changed too much for his liking. I thought he was being a little too dramatic, I thought maybe certain aspects of his job had changed and they probably needed to change in order for his organisation to compete with other organisations. I think this is where having a plan is key; you would anticipate that there might be some kind of change that you might need to take into consideration in the future. This will make you a very flexible person. This is what is going to happen when changes happen in your life: you will understand that you might need to change things in your life. You might also need to learn certain things that you might not have learnt on your way to your dreams.

I asked him if this was what he always wanted to do and he said yes. I remember walking home and thinking that if someone had worked so hard to do what they love, how could a simple company change in practice make them give up what they have worked hard for all their lives? A lot of people think that once they find a job they have been seeking for a long time, it will become plain sailing and everything will work out just the way they want it to. When I successfully resat some of my high school exams, I knew that I had to work hard for my A levels. When I passed them, I knew I had to work hard to pass my degree. After I passed my degree, I knew I had to work hard to find a job. When I found a job, I knew I had to work hard to keep that job.

I have known a lot of people who have worked at something and, just because it was taking a little bit longer than they thought it was going to, they gave up.

You see ladies and gentlemen life is not a sprint; life is a marathon and all you need to do in order for you to win is to cross the finish line. You see, some people will get to that line quicker than others but what matters is that you are able to finish. People who run the marathon do not look at how fast they are going to be or are they going to be faster than anyone else, all they want is to cross the finish line. A lot of people are more bothered about how they are going to do better than other people in class or in their office. When a person is training for a marathon, they do not go through the list and say I should make sure I finish quicker than that person or the other, they only focus on the finishing line.

My advice to you is that you look at your goal each and every day and focus on that alone and not on what other people are doing. A lot of people look at what other people are doing and they end up losing what they have got. I knew a man who had worked very hard in his organisation but then the company brought in a young graduate and he started climbing the ladder quicker than this man. He looked at this and thought he had been here for a long time and not climbed the ladder as quickly as this young man. He was very disappointed and he decided that the best option was to leave the organisation altogether. The day he left one of managers said to him: "It is a shame you are leaving, the boss had so many big plans for you since you had worked so hard for so many years."

So you see, this man was two months away from being one of the senior managers of his organisation and he decided things were not moving fast enough for his liking so he had to move. He has regretted his decision ever since because he has had to start from the beginning again…so close yet so far away. All because he did not have enough patience to wait. You see, when a farmer plants a seed, he does not tell it when to grow;, it grows in its own time and the farmer just has to wait until it's ready. All he has to do is take the weeds out all the time and make sure that the seed is well watered and fertilised. When it's time for harvest, the farmer can enjoy the fruits of his labour. However, if the farmer reaps too early the fruits of his labour will not be what he wants. For example, if seed potatoes are harvested early, all you are going to have is the roots of the sweet potato leaves that you cannot eat. I always say to people that things are going just the way they are supposed to go, even when you cannot see the light at the end of tunnel, you must walk in faith and try and see by faith and not by sight alone. You just have to believe in things that you have not seen and keep going and one day all the answers you want will be given to you. You want to get answers when you reach your goal, not from somebody else telling you that in the future maybe you could have made it if you hadn't given up.

You must always remember that you must keep watering and fertilising the seed if you want to get the results you want. In America, they have a tree called the Chinese bamboo. You have to keep watering this seed for five years for it to come out of the ground. If at any time you stopped watering and fertilising this seed, it will die in the ground. When this seed finally comes out of the ground it grows eighty feet tall (or so it seems) in six weeks. Does a little tree lie dormant for four years and only grow dramatically in the fifth year? The answer is obvious, the tree grows every day when it's being watered and fertilised, and, in the fifth year, you start to see the fruits of the labour. Life is like that: just because you have started, does not mean you will see the results straight away. If you want the results you want you will have to keep going and working at your dream each and every day. If at any point you decide to stop, just like the Chinese bamboo tree, your dream will die in the ground and you will not lead the life you want.

You might not see the results or the skills you are developing at the moment, but in a few years' time you will start seeing the results and you will find that you are able to do things other people cannot do. You have to do things people will not do in order for you to have things other people will not have tomorrow. This one thing people do not do, they work just enough not to get fired, they do not realise that they are not growing at all, and if they do not grow they do not become what they want to be. If they are not what they want to be, they are just existing. Some people died a long time ago; they stopped watering their seed and it died in the ground and they are completely unhappy in their life because of the results they have produced. Remember that when you are working on your dream, you have to work on it every single day and not just now and again. You must engage in constant action every day, you have to do something that will make you get closer to you goal. When the Chinese bamboo tree is watered and fertilised, it takes one step closer to coming out of the ground. Every day that you take a step of coming out of your shadow, you are one step closer to your dream. You have to work hard every day to become what you want to be; nothing in life is given to you free of charge, you will have to work hard for it. You cannot halve the work you have to do, you can never make a deal with life; you have to finish the course and if you do there is always a reward waiting for you.

What if I just cannot see any signs of things changing Frank? There was a young lady I knew in university, I never spoke to her very much because she was in the year above us. My friend who was quite close to her told me how she had lost her parents and her two sisters in one year and here she was doing a degree and a year later a master's. A lot of people used to ask how somebody could do that after losing her entire family. She was a really lovely lady and I really believe that there was not a day that went by without her thinking about her beloved family. I was dying to speak to her and the day I got the chance to speak to her I asked how she has managed to move on with life very quickly and she said: "I would have given up like a lot of people do, but that will not bring my family back. I have realised that death comes unexpectedly so while I am here I might as well do what I can to enjoy life." She also went on to say: "Of course I wish my family were here, I miss them a lot but I have a chance to create a happy life from a sad situation." I looked at her and thought what courage and determination the lady had. This goes to show that we can overcome anything that happens in our lives if we think we can. We can move on without forgetting our loved ones who have passed away.

There was another woman I knew, who I was told had been raped when she was only 16 years of age. This lady was full of life and the joy she produced was untold. When you spoke to her you would have thought she had the best childhood ever, but far from it. She had gone through a lot of trials and she had come out of them a bigger and better person. A woman who has been raped struggles to trust men altogether, but this woman was married and she gladly told her story to anyone who would listen, which I have to say I found really strange. I used to sit there and listen to her and wonder what on earth she was doing. I soon realised she was not trying to make everyone surrounding her feel sorry for her, she was trying to encourage the young people around her to keep moving forward in life. I asked her if she still has trust in men, she said of course she did; some men are bad, but the majority of men are good. She told me that the only reason she is happily married was because she decided to leave her past in the past and embrace what the future had to offer. She focussed on what was good in life and not what was bad in life. If you ask some people how many wrongs have been done to them, they will give you a list pages long. However, if you ask them about the rights that have been done to them, they will struggle to give you three.

You will be walking along, the lights will be turned off, and you will not able to see where you are going, my advice is keep going. I read a poem when I was suffering from depression that made me think, it goes like this: "if you cannot run, walk and if you cannot walk just crawl and whatever happens in your life you must not stop moving forward." You have to keeping moving forward because if you stop, you will stay where you are right now or move back to the life where you were. You have to leave the past in the past because better things await you in the future.

Our ninety-five-year-old neighbour in Newport told me something I will never forget. She said all these years she had prayed for something and always thought that she was waiting for God, but God was waiting for her to make a move to the reward. She looked at everything that had happened in her life in the past and gave up, hence she never got what she wanted. This is the story of so many people...if only they could continue moving forward.

A lot of people give up on their dreams because of the journey; they discover that the journey is harder than they thought it was going to be. There are a lot of things that will happen on the journey and if we do not remain strong we will give up.

My friend hit a road block when she opened her toy shop. The council started doing road works in the street where she was. They were supposed to last three weeks, but three months later they were still going. She was renting the store and because she was not making any money it was no longer financially viable for her to continue running the shop. So, after working hard to open her shop she had to close it. You could be doing very well and things will happen that will change your life forever. What did Libby do? She has continued running her business online and while also doing parties and working with young children with disabilities, which is something that she feels strongly about. One thing about Libby is that she has the love for helping other people and she knew that her business would help a lot of other families. She is now providing a service where children with disabilities can go and enjoy a great time.

Here is a great example of helping other people first in order for you to get what you want. Just finding what other services will be helpful to other people will make you successful in your business. Giving up is never the answer but for a lot of people that's the only option they think they have and so they give up on their dreams. You may have worked really hard but sometimes certain things you do in your life will never work out. You just have to find something else you can do with what you have and where you are. I believe that a lot of people are not successful because they think that if they are to be successful, the first thing they experience should be a success, they think people who are successful in life tried one thing and they made it.

I remember watching a TV programme, *Young Millionaires*, and I was talking to one of my friends about the programme and he said to me that it makes him very depressed when he hears stories about people who are younger than him who are that successful. I think this is true with a lot of people. Imagine you are thirty years of age and you hear of a young person who is ten years your junior who has more money than you can ever think of. When you look at stories like that I would encourage you to look at stories like Steve Jobs, who was fired from the organisation he co-founded because he was not imaginative enough and how people talked him down all the time. Today if you think Apple, you think Steve Jobs. It gets really tough when you are close to your goal but all the troubles you are facing have not come to stay, they have come to pass.

It is hard to live your dreams. It is hard to ask people favours and they turn you away when all you need is someone to help you. It was hard when I went out asking for people to give me work experience and no one was willing. It was hard knowing that my parents did not know anyone who was influential and able to offer me work experience, but I kept looking and knocking on doors anywhere I could find. One day I spent the whole day walking into any organisation I came across to ask if they were willing to take on anyone for work experience. It was a rainy day but I was willing to go to organisation after organisation to ask if they had any positions. I thought that if employers saw a young man going to their business on a very wet day, they would see that that person is willing but I never got anything. In fact some of the staff in some organisations mocked me because I was really soaked because it was raining cats and dogs. I did this because I knew that this was the only way I was going to find what I was looking for. Whenever I get soaked, I am ill for the next two days. People will look at this experience and see it as a very fruitless day but what this told me was the places not to go to next time when I am looking. I kept asking, I asked anyone I thought would know somebody until finally I discovered that one of the people I was with in a male choir was a manager in his company and I asked him for experience. I did not just get work experience, I got paid work experience, which I had never heard of.

Knock and the door shall open and seek and you shall find. These are the words I carried with me in my search. I knew and believed that I was going to find something. So, if the person you thought would help decides not to help, do not throw in the towel, just make sure that you keep going and keep believing that things will work out because they always do in the end. I stand by that statement: things will always work out in the end if you do not give up, and if you give up, things will never work out at all, which is what a lot of people do not realise. You have to keep going and going, and whatever happens, you must keep moving. That is the only way that you are going to learn what you can learn.

If you open a maths text book and you decide you will never learn the stuff and you quit on page one, the chances are you will never learn things on page two or page three or page hundred. However, if you put time in to learning things on page one, no matter how hard you find them, you will get enough confidence to learn things on page two and three and even one hundred. You need to keep growing and moving forward, no matter how bad things get – easy is not an option.

The other reason that you must not give up is that the reward that is waiting is worth it. I was bullied in school and told by some people I was useless and I would never amount to anything, but I kept going. This chapter was written in my own house at the time that a lot of people my age are not able to buy a home, at a time that a lot of people are saying it is hard for young starters to get on the property ladder. I have put myself in this position because I refused to give up; I refused to say that was it for me. I could not see myself as a failure; I was determined that I was going to make something happen. The world saw me as a high school failure, but I saw myself as a new person all together. I was going to be what I wanted to be and nothing was going to stop me. I say to you today, just decide what you want to be and go after it like your life depends on it. Why? Because it does! The hours that I spent studying and reading potential subjects I was going to do for my A Levels paid off in the end and they have made me the person that I am today. Do not focus on all the little worries that people have today, like what latest gadgets they are going to buy or what the latest video game is out or what other people think about you.

Watching Les Brown one morning, I heard him say "do not sweat about small stuff" and by the way it is all small stuff. When people tell you that you will never make it, do not take that to heart – it is all small stuff. When you are laid off from the job you loved and invested so much of your time in, move on – it is small stuff. You have to keep moving forward all the time and go beyond your fears. Do not look at the height you have to jump, just jump and have faith that you are going to make it no matter how hard it is or no matter how bad it gets. If you know what your life work is, just go and do it.

I will not summarise this chapter like I have done with the other chapters but I will end this chapter with a leadership paradox by John Maxwell because I believe that a lot of people do not finish what they started because of what other people say about them. A lot of us would be doing what we were born to do if only our friends or our neighbours did not see something negative about us that we will give up. "People are illogical, unreasonable and self-centred, love them anyway. You do well, and people will accuse you of selfish ulterior motives, do well anyway. If you are successful, you will win false friends and true enemies, but succeed anyway. The good you do today will be forgotten tomorrow, do well anyway. Honesty and frankness makes you vulnerable, be honest and frank anyway. The biggest men with the biggest ideas can be shot down by the smallest of men with the smallest of ideas, think big anyway. People favour underdogs but follow only top dogs, fight for the few underdogs anyway. What you spend years building may be destroyed, build anyway. Some people really do need help but they will attack you if you do, help them anyway. Give the world the best you have and you will get kicked in the teeth, give the world the best you have anyway". Believe in yourself and in your dream and know that you were born to win. If you believe that you only stop when you are done, you are going to *Arise and Shine!*

Chapter 10

Be a Victor

In my introduction to this book I asked a question of how come two people who have gone through exactly the same things in life will achieve different things? How is it that two young people who have been bullied in high school will end up achieving different things in life? One will make it in life and lead a normal life, and the other will not make it. I was bothered by this, why is that certain people who were where I was in 2007 don't seem to have moved on in life? They are doing what they do not like. They feel nothing good is meant to happen to them. They think that the world owes them something because of what they went through. I would like to point out that the world owes you nothing; you do with your life whatever you wish and the world will not care. One day, on one of my bad days, I went to the river that was near our school and something got to me; the river never stopped flowing whether I was happy or sad, it flowed exactly the same. I think this is the same with life. When you are unhappy the world will never stop for you and then start moving when you are happy again, it will continue moving forward and it's up to you to make sure that you do not stand still, because if you do you will never grow. So many people have thought the world will stop for them and they will always run to people if they have the smallest problem. They love the attention that they get from people when things are not going well in their lives hence they will never grow.

You have to be a person who is able to stand on their own. It is nice to have people who are willing to help us when we need help. However, some people have people they literally depend on to lead a happy life and what happens if these people are not there? Their life crumbles to pieces because they do not know how to support themselves. In order for you to *Arise and Shine*, yes you have to have people who support you, but for the majority of the time you must be able to deal with most of the problems that life throws at you. In this chapter, I am going to show you how people destroy their lives without knowing that they are doing so.

A lot of people look at the wrongs that have been done to them and they think that people should be there all the time to feel sorry for them. In school I had a friend who had a lot going on in his life but he wanted all of us to feel sorry for him. He would tell us everything that was going on in his life, he would tell anyone who was willing to listen. A lot of people struggle to fit in anywhere because of the victim mentality, they want people to treat them differently or specially. They become people who complain about anything and everything that is going wrong in their lives. They seem to have something to complain about, if it is not one thing then it is another. This is what happened to our friend; whenever we decided to go out he was the last to be asked out because we all could not stand his moaning about something again and again. It is true that we are all self-made and the more we complain about all our problems, the more we are creating the person people will not listen to and the harder we will find it to get on with people.

You see, if you are always complaining about the troubles in your life, you will not have time to listen to your friends. We all like to be heard and if you are not listening to your friends, they will not listen to you. You become a selfish person and people will see that and will not associate with you. You might be a lovely person but the fact that you are always going on about things that are not working out in your life will not make you sound like a good person. I have met people who have the greatest wrongs done to them yet they do not spend all day and all night telling you about it. They tell you about the good things that have happened in their lives and what they are doing next. They go out to help people who are going through the same circumstances and cope with whatever it is. Sue was the wife of one of the cancer patients who came regularly to our department. She used to make sure she checked how everyone was doing and she used to spread joy around the department. Her husband was happily sat in the corner and they never ever complained about what was going on and they were happy about the good news of everyone else.

If you see yourself as a victim, you will never see yourself as a person who was born to win, simple as that. If you see yourself as a victim, you will see yourself as a person who is fighting against the world. An older lady was brought to work in our department; she was very slow she never seemed to understand things at all. I remember saying that you can teach her until you are blue in the face she will not have a clue what you are on about. After a few weeks she discovered that she was struggling so did she ask for help? No. Instead she played the victim card; she went around telling anyone who could listen that I wasn't teaching her anything. This was of course not true—she was struggling—and the job was not as easy as she thought it was going to be. Here is a lady who could have just asked for help, but before anyone could discover that she was struggling, she went on the defensive straight away.

Victims always want to have the upper hand even when they are in the wrong. However, they do not realise that mistakes happen every day and they are part and parcel of life. If anyone tells you that they have never made a mistake in their lives, they are lying to you. Mistakes happen to everyone and we should learn from them and move on. However, if we are covering them up then we will never learn from them; if we do not learn from them, we will never grow; if we do not grow, we are never going to be happy; if we are not happy, what else is there? You must always look at what you are doing to learn in your life; whatever has happened, has happened, and the world does not owe you anything. Imagine if your friend says you owe them money and you are certain you don't, the chances are that you are probably not going to give them any money at all unless you give it to them to keep the peace. So, if you go out acting like the world owes you something, I have some news for you my friend, it doesn't, and you will get nothing from it. The only way that you can get something from it is if you plant the seed of success, only then will you reap success. I say stop seeing yourself as a victim, find out what you don't know in life and go out and learn it. To be where I am today, I needed to go out and learn what I did not know, this was the only wayI knew that was going to give me what I wanted.

Wrongs had been done in the past but I was not going to run around to people and ask them to give me an apology, I had no time for that – I had a dream! I was no longer a victim of bullying I was a victor! I had a dream to protect; I had something to work for every day. I had so much to learn, so much so that I did not look around me for support, but I found in when I began the journey. If you want to be successful in life, you have to move forward and look at your problem as something that you can overcome. Do not look at what you are now or what you have, think of the person you would become if you stopped feeling sorry for yourself and embraced life for what it is. I have had a lot of trials and tribulations on the way to where I am now but I have never looked back; I have always looked ahead to what is to come. I want to enjoy the beauty of life and not worry about things that might go wrong.

If you are a victor, you will know that you were born to enjoy life and not to just throw it away with trepidation. Two women discovered that their husbands were cheating on them; one decided that after the divorce she was going to move on and enjoy life. Her ex-husband moved and married another woman. But that does not bother her because she knows what she wants in life and she is happy just bringing up her children. When the weekend comes, she is happy when he takes the children because that will give her a well-deserved break. She puts her feet up, lights a candle, has a nice glass of red wine and puts on her favourite music and bliss at last. The children come back Sunday evening, and she does not ask the children how they spent every minute of the day because she loves the fact her children have a relationship with their father, so for her it is a win-win situation.

However, on the other side we have the other women who will tell anyone who is willing to listen to her about how she was cheated on and how her husband is a bad person and how she wishes something bad would happen to him. She complains about how she has to deal with her children every day of the week on her own. However, when her husband comes and gets the kids for the weekend, she is jealous and wants to know what they did, which makes the children feel guilty for even going to spend time with their father and his new partner and the kids are unhappy.

What is going on here then? The first woman has understood that life is what happens when everything seems to be going well. She has accepted what has happened and she is willing to move on and allow her children to have a relationship with their father. When her children go off, she sees it as a time to refresh her mind and think about what she wants for herself. Remember: we become what we think about. She spends that time thinking and putting positive things in her mind and she is able to build her life. When she has the children, she does not have time to think about herself, all she thinks about is her children. However, when she gets an opportunity to be on her own, she makes sure she spends it happily and thoughtfully. On the other hand, the other woman spends the whole week looking after her children and she just wishes she could have a break. However, when the opportunity to have a break does come, she is still not happy. She wakes up to the fact that her kids are spending time with her ex and his new partner. She is so worked up that she cannot even sleep. Before she knows it, the kids are back and it's back to the busy week regime.

A victor will always be thinking about the big things in life. They will always think about what will make them grow and what will make them happy. They will enjoy their time with family because they will understand that they are supposed to give out love before they can get it back. This reminds me of a song I loved that we used to sing when we were young: *'Love is never love until you give it away'*. Some people will be like the second woman who will be worrying about what her ex is doing and what he is doing with his kids. Two women: one thinking big thoughts, the other sweating small stuff because they had chosen to be a victim.

Imagine that your house was on fire, would you just stand there and watch it burn to ashes or are you going to try to save as much as you can from it and try and put the fire out? A lot of people have a small fire that has started in their house and if they do not put it out, they will soon be engulfed and it will be impossible to put it out. When I failed my high school exam, I had a fire burning in my life that needed to be put out and the only way I could put that fire out was to have a dream and goal to aim for: I needed to have purpose. Some people told me that I did the best I could in the circumstances; I joined high school halfway through, I was always going to struggle, and English is not even my first language so I must have done really well. There are so many excuses in that sentence, and that is how people who are victims operate. They try to find an excuse for why they are not doing very well. In order for you to be successful, you have to stop looking for excuses for why something failed and look at how you can fix it. I had failed my high school exam, but I did not need anyone to make me feel better; I knew what I needed to do to make a success out of my life and that was all I needed.

You hear so many excuses: I had this and that going on in my life; I was not very well, when I was writing an exam; my cousin passed away. And so on. People will tell you anything to explain why they have not made it in life. I listen to these stories and think to myself: that was eight years ago, I am sure you could have done something about that. However, if you ask them about it, they will then give you yet another excuse. They will tell you about other things that happened in their lives to stop them from achieving their goals. Well, life is not all sunshine; if you are looking for perfect conditions, I have got news – I am afraid you will never find it.

Sometimes we will find ourselves in circumstances that we did not expect but we have got a choice. We can either be the people that tell the success story, or the people that come up with the excuses for why we did not make it in life. All we are doing is making ourselves victims of circumstances when we can be victors of circumstances. All we need to do to be victors of circumstances is look for solutions and not problems. We should not look at what other people are doing but aim to fix it. In my current job, I find that people will always look at whoever made the mistake before they fix it. Do not be a problem finder, become a problem fixer and refuse to be a victim of circumstances

I have an eye condition called Nystagmus, which causes my eyes to move constantly and I make mistakes that a lot of people do not make. I did not know that people with my condition cannot play sport until I was diagnosed. I played sport regardless, as well as a lot of other things that the doctors say that people with my condition cannot do – I did it all. When I found out what I had, a lot of people were telling me what disability benefits were there for me and who I could speak to. I could have forgotten everything I leant about myself in the previous year and just said that I was going to struggle. I said to myself: I have this condition, I will never drive in my life, which was a heartbreak for me.

I knew that when I found employment it would have to be in a place that I can easily get to by public transport. I struggle to even read the notice boards on the train station. It has been a struggle which I have kept to myself, which has been hard. However, I refused to let it keep me from what I love doing. I do not go to bed and think about it or wake up in the morning and think about it. It rarely crosses my mind because I have looked at what is around me and I have realised that I have got a lot of important things to think about. Moreover, I think I am blessed to live in a country were employers are required to adjust to the conditions of their employees, thank the Lord for that. I worked for a person I knew through my fiancée and I really struggled and he decided he was going to let me go. I knew that my eyesight was my problem but did that stop me from looking to do something that I loved doing; no way, it was not going to be over until I won. I hear a lot of people say they cannot do this and that because they have such-and-such condition; they have made themselves to be victims of their conditions, whereas I refused to be a victim of my condition. I have worked in my current role just short of a year and I have done well despite my eye condition. Instead of telling yourself what you cannot do because of your condition, ask yourself a different question: what can you do despite your condition? There is always something that you can do better than you expect. Remember you do not have to be great to get started, you have to get started to be great.

I heard someone say: focus on the promise and not the problem; if you work hard at something you will grow. Einstein once said: "Unless you do something beyond that which you have mastered you will never grow." If you look at your medical condition and limit yourself to what you can do you will never grow. Les Brown said: "Aim for the moon because if you miss you will just land on the stars." I looked for the job that was going to suit my eye condition and I found it. Les Brown said something in his video that I found interesting: "The thing that you are seeking is seeking you." I came into this world with nystagmus, but the creator also made me with something that I will be able to do very well, despite my condition. The best way you will go from being a victim to a victor is if you are able to count your blessings one by one. I have worked with people in my current job who have perfect vision, but I am still able to do the job as good if not better than them because I am a victor.

Being black, I have come across people who have judged me very quickly before they even got to know me, it has become part of being black. However, I believe that the majority of people are good people, I believe that people in general are good. I believe that I am part of a very lucky generation who live in a more equal society than any other generation. We are all self-made but only the successful will admit it. A few weeks ago, I was walking home from the train station when I saw a few black youths causing trouble in the street. When somebody pointed out that what they were doing was not good they said: "Is it because we are black?" I remember thinking to myself: no, it is because what you are doing is illegal. I had to ask myself one question, how come black people are the ones who struggle to fit in anywhere more than most?

I think it's because we have all this history and we are always going to go back to it. Some people genuinely do not like you because you are black, but, to most people, this is not very important anymore. A lot of young black people will tell you it is hard to find employment, but have you ever asked them if they have enrolled on extra training courses so that they can get an advantage on the competition? I was surprised with the number of young black men who were on my course when I was at university, the majority of whom were international students – and I could count the local students with one hand easily.

I think a lot of people have made themselves victims of their race when all they are doing is failing to compete with other people. What we put in life, we are going to produce nothing more and nothing less. Certain doors will shut in our faces, but as long as we keep going, we are going to find what we are looking for. For a lot of people race is just an excuse for them to go and do all the illegal things that they want. I said earlier that life is a river of success and you can get as much as you want out of it – it's up to you. You may be part of the minority in society, but as long as you have a desire to win and a desire to help other people get what they want, you are going to make it. As long as you look for excuses why you will not make it, you will fail in life. You will not get anything out of it. How people will be looking back in a few years' time and realising that they were not victims and that they had a lot of opportunities, more than our fathers ever had. Look for the life you want, do not focus on things victimising you, always focus on things that will give you victory.

I do, however, believe that some people would rather be victims than victors because the pleasure of having people rallying around them when things are not going well is a lot greater than anything that they have at present. People who have parents who did everything for them, for example, lack in confidence because things have always been done for them by their parents. You will see the house of an adult who has had everything done for them the minute you walk through the door. A lot of parents think that this is the only way that they will show love to their children; they do not realise that the greatest act of love that a parent can give to his or her children is the ability to cope with life. Life is not easy, easy is not an option. If everything is done for the child, the parent is creating an illusion that life is all sunshine, which it is not. Life will beat you down to your knees. You might cuddle your child when they do something wrong, the world will not do that. You have to teach them a life lesson; you have to let them know that there are certain things in life that you will not just get away with. You see, if all a parent has done in life is avoiding criticising the child, when they get into the real world they will not cope at all.

We are living in a fast-moving world where a lot of people are watching what you are doing; if you are slow, you are left behind; if the business you are working in gets into financial difficulties, you will be one of the first ones to go. How is that fair? Imagine you are on a sinking ship. The crew will always throw away the things that they think have no value at all, so if you are not bringing any value to the business you will be among the first people to go. You see, victims do not look at what they can do for the organisation they are working in; victims look to see what the organisation can do for them. Working with a lady who was not pulling her weight taught me something about victims: they expect a lot after putting in very little. Breaking news: what you put in is what you get out. In other words, help other people get what they want in life and you will get what you want.

People will tell you about everything that has gone wrong in their life, they are living in their past each and every day. My brother and I have completely different tastes in life. Sometimes I have sat there and watched one of his favourite movies and I have to say I have not enjoyed some of them and have really hated some of them. I have not gone back and watched the ones that I have hated because I did not want to see them again; I want to see something nice that will give me joy. I believe our life is like a movie, but, unlike a movie, we can decide how the ending is going to be.

If you do not like where life is going, change it: do something about it to get the results that you want. If you work in sales and you are not hitting the sales target, make more phone calls and you will change the results that you want. If you are struggling in the workplace, request training: do whatever you need to do to change the circumstance of your life. Victims do not look at how they can change their lives because they keep playing the old movies where they failed in the past.

I spoke about the woman who did really well in life despite being raped as a young woman, how did she do this? She did not want to play the old movie, she wanted to create something that she will enjoy for the rest of her life. However, a lot of people will always look back at what happened in the past and they allow it to destroy their future as well. I knew a woman who was married to an overpowering husband, which meant that she could not see her parents very often. When her daughter married a lovely young man, who loved her dearly and respected her and would not stop her from seeing her own parents, the mother could have learned a lot from their marriage because of what happened in the past but the marriage did not work out in the end. This is all because the mother was being a victim of circumstances she was playing the video from the past and she did not want to let it go. This resulted in her daughter and her husband arguing about the same things over and over again; she refused so see the kindness and love the young man had for her daughter because of what happened in the past.

I always say to people: look at what the past has taught you about life, pick all the positives from it and leave the negative things there because they do not bring any good to your future. You might understand that people are not the same, so if a man or woman did wrong to you in the past, that does not mean that all people will do wrong to you. If you had a boss who was not good to you, you must let go of that because there is always going to be another boss who is going to be good to you.

You can go from being a victim to being a victor by focusing on the good things about life, things that you are able to do that others cannot do. In other words, count your blessings one by one each day when you get out bed, getting out of bed is a blessing in itself. You are able to read this book; there are a lot of people who are not able to read this book because they are blind and would love to be where you are right now.

The people who make it in life are people who look for positives in everything that is going on in their life. I believe that a lot of people focus too much on what is going wrong in their lives rather than the good that is going on in their lives. There is always going to be something bad in your life and if you decide to look for it, you will find it. Too many people are going out every day looking for what is wrong in their lives. They focus so much on what is going wrong in their lives that they lose sight of all the things that are going right. I think a lot of people think that the world is supposed to love them so much so they do not love themselves for who they are. You can easily turn your life from being a victim to a victor, here are some of the steps that helped me.

1. You must always associate pain with being a victim. I believe that a lot of people have decided to be victims of their circumstances because they love the attention that it brings and they do not want to give it up. I remember that a few people I

told about being bullied in school would automatically feel sorry for me and they would invite me to come to parties and for this, that and the other. I realised that I was not making real friends, they were just people who felt sorry for me and did not think much about me when I was not there. I associated being a victim with being a painful experience; I wanted to change my life and do something great so that people could see that I was a strong person who could stand on his own. I made real friends and I was a lot happier. I really believed that I was as good as the best students we had in university. Whereas when I was being a victim, I believed the majority of people where better than me. I suddenly realised that I was better than good. I was the kid who was bullied in high school, but I am here with a chance to achieve dreams. I decided to be a great example to other people to show that everything is possible when you don't see yourself as a victim anymore. I wanted to be seen as a great overcomer and some people remember me as that. I decided that there was too much pain in being a victim and so much pleasure and potential in being a victor.

2. You must make sure that you create the life that you want. A lot of people are living the life that was made for them by their circumstances. Bad things are going to happen the good the bad and the evil. However, if we can take control of our lives, we are going to live happy lives. Many people believe they have no choices in life, but— consciously or unconsciously—we are making choices every day of our lives. We should make an

effort to ensure that we are making choices consciously and that we are creating the movie that we would want to see over and over again. Imagine if somebody was going to watch your movie decades later, how would they feel? Are they going to look at it once and throw it away and never see it again? Or are they going to be looking at it thinking that, no matter how bad things are or how bad they will get, they are going to make it? You have to make a decision today. Pause for a second and ask yourself these three questions and honestly answer them. Where have you been? Where are you now? Where you are going? Answer these questions and decide where you want to take your life

3. Whatever you do in life, do it as if your life depended on it! Why? Because it does. In order to be happy, you have to make sure that you are doing something that you love. When you look at your dream, look at it as something that God put you here to do. That's the reason for your existence and nothing else. A lot of people go to jobs that they are not happy in and they work there for decades because they are afraid of doing that one thing that they were born to do. A lot of people do not fulfil their dreams because they have been told in the past over and over again that they are not good enough. Well, you do not have to be great to get started, you have to get started to become great. For a lot of parents, their existence depends on the health of their children. I remember when my mum went months without pay, she had to make sure that we were still fed

and sometimes she went without food herself so that we could have some because we were her happiness. For who I am and what I am, I owe it to my mother for all she did for us and what she keeps doing in our lives. If you have a dream, go after it because that is the thing that will bring you happiness. However, you must remember that happiness is not about the physical things that you have: happiness is an emotional and deeper than wealth. It is not what you get, it is who you become as a result of achieving your goals that is important.

4. You must make sure that you plant positive things in your mind. What we all become is what we think about. We are where we are and what we are because of what goes into our minds. The good thing about life is we can change who we are and what we are by changing what goes into our minds. How do we do this? We must associate ourselves with winners at all times. People who are always looking at what they can achieve tomorrow and not looking at what could have been yesterday. Doing this will not make us motivated at all and we will live mediocre lives. If we do not plant what we want in our minds, the things that we do not want will grow there. Let us look at what we are watching or what music we listen to. Just like the song with the lyrics, 'The worst you ever gave me was the best you have gave me'. Good things are supposed to happen to you and if you really believe this, good things will happen to you.

5. You must make sure that you set your bars high. Victims always set their bars really low and they

always achieve them. They may complain about how bad life is for them but this is because they have set their bars so low and they have hit. If you want to become a chairman of a company, but you do not put in extra hours you are out of the office at 5pm exactly every day, the chances are you will never be the chairman of your organisation. You have to make sure that you dream big because if you can dream it, you can do it. Decide that you are going to go for what you want in life; associate great pain with the past and great pleasure with the future that is to come. Look at what you want and go after it as if your life depended on it. Decide that you are not going to live by watching the old movie of your life, but you are going to start making a new movie with a glorious ending. Whilst a lot of people are reading their history, other people are writing new scripts with a glorious ending. You only live once even though some people live their lives like it is a dress rehearsal. Always aim for the moon because even if you miss, you will just land on the stars!

Life is meant to be enjoyed. You might have failed in the past but that does not matter anymore. People I know now do not even know that I once was a high school failure because all they have ever known is a university graduate. You are truly better than good and better than most so live your dreams! May the Lord bless you and keep you and make his face shine upon you and be gracious unto you. You have got what it takes, so go and do what you were born to do and you will *Arise and Shine*!

References

Anthony Robbins (n.d.) Awaken the sleeping Giant within,: . Earl Nightingale (n.d.) Lead the Field , : . Earl Nightingale (n.d.) The Strangest Secret, : . John Maxwell (n.d.) 5 Levels of leadership, : . John Maxwell, : . Les Brown (n.d.) It's Not Over Until You Win, : . Les Brown (n.d.) Live Your Dreams, : . Susan Jeffers (n.d.) Feel the fear and do it anyway, Zig Ziglar (n.d.) Born to Win, : . Zig Ziglar (n.d.) See You At The Top

Lightning Source UK Ltd.
Milton Keynes UK
UKHW01f0109160818
327295UK00001B/4/P